SHORT WALF

Staffordshire Pubs

Nick Channer

COUNTRYSIDE BOOKS
NEWBURY, BERKSHIRE

COUNTRYSIDE BOOKS
3 Catherine Road
Newbury, Berkshire

ISBN 1 85306 417 3

Designed by Mon Mohan
Cover illustration by Colin Doggett
Photographs by the author
Maps by Jack Street

Produced through MRM Associates Ltd., Reading
Printed by Woolnough Bookbinding Ltd., Irthlingborough

Contents

Area map showing the locations of the walks.

Publisher's Note

We hope that you obtain considerable enjoyment from this book; great care has been taken in its preparation. However, changes of landlord and actual closures are sadly not uncommon. Likewise, although at the time of publication all routes followed public rights of way or permitted paths, diversion orders can be made and permissions withdrawn.

We cannot of course be held responsible for such diversion orders and any inaccuracies in the text which result from these or any other changes to the routes nor any damage which might result from walkers trespassing on private property. However, we are anxious that all details covering the walks and the pubs are kept up to date and would therefore welcome information from readers which would be relevant to future editions.

Introduction

I often find that whenever the county of Staffordshire crops up in conversation, those people who are not familiar with its attractions and its distinctive character often ask me what on earth it has to offer anyone. For years, of course, it was inextricably linked with the grime of industry when the chimneys of the Potteries and the Black Country spewed out filthy smoke.

The image is now much cleaner and greener and these days this much underrated county, which lies at the very heart of England, has much to attract and entertain the visitor. Staffordshire's natural beauty is surprisingly diverse and abundant, but it is in the north of the county, in the Staffordshire Moorlands and the Southern Peak District, that it can be seen at its most dramatic. Here, you can explore a rugged landscape of emerald green hills, craggy limestone cliffs and deep, narrow valleys. The romance of hidden caves and age-old caverns add to the charm of the area.

A perfect way to discover parts of the county is to use the old, long abandoned railway lines, which have been skilfully converted into footpaths and cycle trails. However, it is not just the legacy of the railway era that has been put to good use. Staffordshire lies at the centre of an intricate network of inland waterways and the county offers many miles of towpaths running alongside these delightful old transport routes, giving a fascinating insight into the area's industrial past.

As well as exploring canals and disused railways, the walks in this book take you to the remote corners of the county, to the fertile farmland of mid-Staffordshire and to the lovely woodland expanses of Cannock Chase. There are also strolls in the beautiful Churnet valley and along sections of the Staffordshire Way, a long distance footpath which runs from Mow Cop on the Cheshire border to Kinver Edge at the southern tip of the county.

Each walk starts and finishes at a local pub. Mostly, the inns are traditional hostelries, though one or two are modern town pubs or roadhouses. As far as the inns go, there is hopefully something for everyone. All the pubs serve food and welcome families and walkers; many having good facilities for children. Unless otherwise stated, permission has been granted to park at the inn whilst doing the walk. Details of the menu, times of opening and when food is served are also included.

The sketch maps that accompany each of the walks are designed to guide you to the starting point and give an overview of the routes. For proper detail and scale, Ordnance Survey maps are recommended – the relevant sheet numbers are provided in each chapter.

As a safeguard, I would urge you to carry some basic waterproof clothing on the walk, just in case the weather changes. Good walking shoes or boots are also recommended – even on the very short routes.

At the end of each chapter, there are suggestions for places to visit in the vicinity of the walk – museums, historic houses, reservoirs and the like – so that, if you wish, you can make a whole day of it.

Finally, I hope the walks and the inns in this book give you a flavour of Staffordshire. With its variety of landscape and its many characteristic features, it is a county worth getting to know.

Nick Channer
Spring 1996

1 Mow Cop
The Ash Inn

The hilltop village of Mow Cop is a wild place littered with rocky outcrops of millstone grit and often completely enveloped by mist and low cloud – as I have discovered each time I have been there. Its steep streets of sturdy buildings overlook two counties, Staffordshire and Cheshire, and on a good day you can see the Peak District, Manchester, Shropshire and even parts of Wales. The Ash Inn can be found on the east side of Mow Cop, on the lower slopes of the village. There is a lot of land at the rear of the pub, including a playing field and a children's recreational area.

As well as the lounge and carvery, there is a popular menu which caters for everyone – bar snacks include soup of the day, jacket potatoes, sandwiches and salads. For something more substantial there are several steaks, including grilled sirloin, beef curry, grilled trout, fillet of plaice, breaded haddock and chicken Kiev. There is a choice of vegetarian dishes and a selection of chef's specials – battered cod and beef in Guinness are examples of what you might find available. The Ash Inn also has a children's menu and on

Sunday there is a traditional roast lunch. Theakston Best Bitter, Tetley Bitter and Marston's Pedigree are the hand-pulled beers; there are several lagers – Castlemaine XXXX, Carlsberg, Skol – as well as Guinness and Olde English draught cider.

The pub is open from 11.30 am to 4 pm and 6.30 pm to 11 pm Monday to Friday, 11.30 am to 11 pm on Saturday and 12 noon to 10.30 pm on Sunday. Food is available from 12 noon to 2 pm and 6.30 pm to 9.30 pm Monday to Friday, 12 noon to 2 pm and 6.30 pm to 10 pm on Saturday and 12 noon to 8.30 pm on Sunday. Large parties should book at the weekend. No dogs please.

Telephone: 01782 513167.

How to get there: Follow the A34 between Stoke-on-Trent and Congleton and follow the signs for Mow Cop. Pass a well known local pub, the Cheshire View, and turn right at the next T-junction. Descend Chapel Bank to the next junction, then bear right and the inn will be seen on the left after a short distance.

Parking: The Ash Inn has its own car park. Alternatively, use the car park at Mow Cop.

Length of the walk: 2¼ miles. Map: OS Landranger 118 Stoke-on-Trent and Macclesfield (inn GR 856568).

This is more of a village heritage trail than a country ramble. The unusual village of Mow Cop, perched in the sky and famous as the birthplace of Primitive Methodism, is a fascinating place to explore on foot. The views are tremendous and the changing weather conditions often give Mow Cop a unique, almost eerie atmosphere.

The Walk
Turn right on leaving the inn, walk along the road, pass several turnings, including Hillside Close, and go on past Blue Flame Autos. Follow the road between lines of houses and look for a church tower up ahead. Keep the church in view and continue into Congleton Road. Pass a turning to Tunstall, then as you draw level with the church, turn left and go up a flight of steps between bungalows. After a few yards the path forks; take the right turning, ascend to the higher ground, then cross a stile and go out to the road by a bungalow. Turn left and follow the road between houses

9

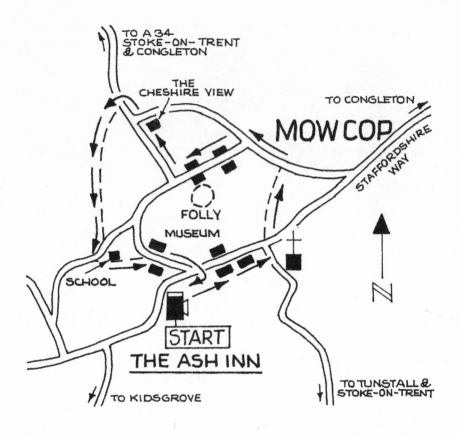

and cottages, climbing even higher now. Further on, the lane descends a little and passes a sign for the South Cheshire Way, a long distance path of some 31 miles (53 km) extending to Grindley Brook on the Cheshire/Shropshire border. There is also a sign for the Staffordshire Way, which starts at Mow Cop and heads south through the county.

Continue along the road and turn left into the High Street. Pass the entrance to Mow Cop, a classic ruined folly built on a rocky summit, 1100 feet above sea level, by a local man, Randle Wilbraham, in 1754 as a romantic eye-catcher. This prominent landmark has been photographed on numerous occasions over the years – most memorably when it is silhouetted against the evening sky. At 6 am on Sunday 31st May 1807, a field not far from this spot became the venue for an open air camp meeting which lasted 12 hours and led ultimately to the birth of Primitive Methodism in 1812. Ten thousand Methodists attended a service here in 1937 when the National Trust acquired Mow Cop.

Returning to the walk, continue along High Street as far as Top Station Road. Take the turning, cross the county boundary into Cheshire and begin to descend very steeply. In front of you are glorious, far-reaching views to the west. Pass Primitive Street, which takes its name from Mow Cop's historic associations with Primitive Methodism, and on the right is the Cheshire View public house. Just beyond it, opposite Wood Street, turn left at the public footpath sign and follow the rutted driveway, with impressive views across Cheshire on your right. Pass a line of bungalows and houses and continue on the track until you reach the road.

Go straight on into Church Street and pass the Church of St Luke on the right. Opposite the church is Woodcocks Well Church of England School, a solid stone building dated 1858. Keep to the road, then as it begins to bend right, turn sharp left by the entrance to number 45 (Rockside) and go up the bank, with the road now parallel on your left. After a few yards the path curves to the right and proceeds over some rough grassland From here there are magnificent views ahead of you into Staffordshire and behind you across Cheshire. Follow the path as it bends left and continues up by a bungalow to join a track. Keep ahead with a stone wall on your left and pass between stone-built houses and bungalows. Turn right at the road and pass the entrance to Mow Cop's Chapel Museum, housed in an old Wesleyan Chapel. The theme of the museum is social history and there are various exhibitions and displays. The birth of Primitive Methodism and the development of the Sunday School movement are included and you can also learn about millstone quarrying in the area. Follow the road down to the junction and bear sharp right back to the inn.

Places of interest nearby
Mows Cop's Chapel Museum is open from May to September, Wednesday to Friday 2 pm to 5 pm, Saturday and bank holidays 11 am to 6 pm and Sunday 2 pm to 6 pm. *Biddulph Grange Garden* is owned by the National Trust and includes an Egyptian Court, a Chinese pagoda and an Italian garden. The 15-acre garden has been superbly restored by the National Trust. Telephone: 01782 517999.

2 Longnor
The Crewe and Harpur Arms

Longnor, with its bustling square and streets of stone houses, was once a thriving market town. Even today this windswept village, sandwiched between the rivers Manifold and Dove and only ½ mile from the Derbyshire border, has a real sense of community spirit about it. The Crewe & Harpur Arms is mid-19th century and once belonged to the Harper Crewe estate, which stretched for miles and included many farms and other properties in the area. The pub, where tenants came to pay their rent, was sold off by the family about 20 years ago.

Food is served every day and includes a good selection of dishes. Among the starters are crispy garlic mushrooms and home-made soup of the day; main meals include grilled sirloin, mixed grill (sirloin, gammon, liver, chop, burgers, sausage and black pudding), deep-fried plaice with lemon, lasagne, steak and kidney pie and cheese, ham or mushroom omelette. There are Indian and Chinese dishes, salads, sandwiches, toasties and sweets. There is a specials board, a popular children's menu and a traditional roast lunch is served on Sunday. Marston's Pedigree, Best Bitter and a guest beer are the real ales on hand pump. McEwan's and Foster's are the lagers available, and there is also Murphy's stout and Woodpecker cider on draught.

The Crewe & Harpur Arms, which is also a hotel, offers accommodation in 7 bedrooms (4 family rooms) and features a restaurant (larger parties advised to book), morning coffee from 9.30 am and afternoon tea. There is also a beer garden with children's play area. Well behaved dogs are allowed in the bar. The bar is open from 11 am to 3 pm (2 pm in winter) and 6 pm to 11 pm (7 pm in winter) Monday to Saturday and 12 noon to 10.30 pm on Sunday . Food is served from 11 am to 2 pm and 7 pm to 9.30 pm Monday to Saturday and 12 noon to 3 pm and 6 pm to 9 pm on Sunday.

Telephone: 01298 83205.

How to get there: Follow the A523 between Leek and Ashbourne and then head north on the B5053 towards Buxton. Drive into the village of Longnor and the inn is on the right.

Parking: There is room to park at the pub, or in the village if you prefer.

Length of the walk: 2¼ miles. Map: OS Landranger 119 Buxton, Matlock and Dove Dale (inn GR 087648).

From the picturesque village of Longnor, the walk cuts across country to the banks of the Manifold river. As you follow the riverside path, there are pretty views over the Staffordshire Moorlands.

The Walk
Opposite the pub is the Longnor Craft Centre which is worth a closer look. Note the tariff above the main entrance – a relic from the days when this historic, late 19th- century building was the market hall. For many years it was the focal point of Longnor and served as the local community centre, where dances were held every week. By the late 1970s the building was in a poor state of repair and much work was required to renovate and restore it before it became the studio of a local sculptor. The nearby church is

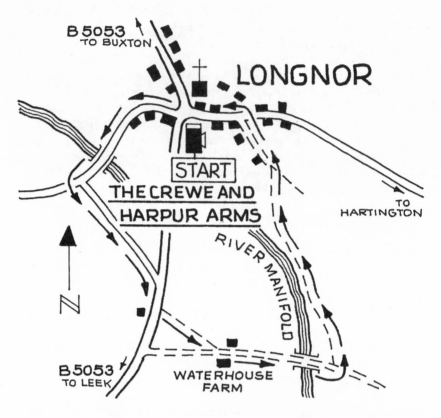

B 5053
TO BUXTON

LONGNOR

START
THE CREWE AND
HARPUR ARMS

TO
HARTINGTON

RIVER MANIFOLD

N

B 5053
TO LEEK

WATERHOUSE
FARM

dedicated to St Bartholomew and medieval fairs were once held in
the churchyard. A local legend suggests that it was considered bad
luck if the church clock struck 3 during a funeral service. Many
believed that should the clock chime, another death would soon
take place. As the years went by, arrangements were put in hand to
halt the clock if it was thought the funeral service would be a long
one. Longnor is still remembered for an incident during the Second
World War. Several enemy planes dropped bombs on the parish,
partly destroying a church in the neighbourhood.

   With the Longnor Craft Centre in front of you, turn left and
cross the B5053. Take the road signposted Leek and Royal Cottage
and follow it as it bends left. Pass between rows of stone cottages,
then leave the village and head out into the countryside. Cross a

footpath on the left and go over the stone road bridge spanning the river Manifold. Take the next left turning and follow the narrow, single-track lane between dry-stone walls. The buildings of Longnor can clearly be seen up on the hill and all around you are views of the Peak District and the wild, gritstone hills of the Staffordshire Moorlands.

Continue to the junction with the B5053 and turn right. Follow the road up the gentle slope to draw level with a house on the right. Bear left into the field and cross it diagonally to the far corner. Ahead of you are very good views across the Manifold valley and on the right is the jagged ridge of the southern Peak. Pass through the squeeze-stile and head diagonally across the field to join a track on the far side. Follow the track through a field boundary and down the slope towards Waterhouse Farm. Pass between the farmhouse and outbuildings and go straight on over the river Manifold to cross a cattle-grid. After about 70 yards you reach a stile on the left and one on the right. Take the left-hand path and cross the field to a stile in the hedgerow. Follow the path across several field boundaries to the river bank, cross a footbridge and continue with the river on your left.

Head across the next enclosure to a stile and continue to the next stile. Keep the river on your left and walk alongside a line of trees, which screen the river. Continue for about 100 yards towards a dry-stone wall and then veer half-right to a squeeze-stile in the wall. A sign requests that you keep in single file. Follow the path up the slope, keeping to the right of some farm buildings. With the houses of Longnor now visible, make for the left corner of the enclosure and cross into the next pasture, then go diagonally up the slope to a gate leading into the farm. Pass between the outbuildings, turn right in front of the house and follow the drive to the road. Bear left, pass the Cheshire Cheese Hotel and the Manifold Tearoom and return to the inn.

Places of interest nearby
Tittesworth Reservoir includes a landscaped picnic area, barbecue, cafeteria, visitor centre and children's play area. There are also walks along the water's edge, which should appeal to the ornithologist. *Rooke's Pottery* at Hartington offers an original range of terracotta garden pots and decorative heads of animals, birds and humans. Telephone: 01298 84650.

③ Stanley
The Travellers Rest

Stanley is a very attractive hilltop village of stone houses and cottages. At one time it was known as Stoneleigh, meaning stony ground, and it is thought that the Earls of Derby hailed from here. The Travellers Rest is a charming old inn – appropriately named for those undertaking a walk in the area before relaxing over some liquid refreshment! The pub originally comprised 2 cottages and a slaughterhouse, but try not to let that put you off your food! It certainly fails to deter customers, as the inn is always full to the brim with diners. The pub's interior is very attractive and cosy, featuring beams, horse brasses and exposed stone walls.

The lunchtime menu highlights various starters – soup, pâté and toast, garlic mushrooms, egg mayonnaise – and main courses like chicken curry, chilli con carne, cheese and ham quiche, deep-fried breaded scampi and steak and kidney pie. There are also ploughman's lunches, jacket potatoes and a selection of sandwiches, including cheese, coleslaw and chilli. Some dishes are available in the evening as well, such as lasagne verdi, salmon and broccoli bake, chicken Kiev and fillet, sirloin and T-bone steak. The pub offers a range of sweets and children have their own menu. Marston's Pedigree and Best Bitter and Morland Old Speckled Hen are the real ales available on hand pump. There is Heineken and Becks Bier for the lager drinker, Red Rock for the cider enthusiast and a varied wine list.

The Travellers Rest does not take bookings and dogs are restricted to the garden only. The bar is open from 12 noon to 2.30 pm and 7 pm to 11 pm Monday to Saturday and 12 noon to 3 pm and 7 pm to 10.30 pm on Sunday. Food is served every day from 12 noon to 2 pm and 7 pm to 9.30 pm.

Telephone: 01782 502580.

How to get there: Follow the A53 between Stoke-on-Trent and Leek and head south at Endon into Station Road, near the junction with the B5051, following the signs for Stanley. Drive up through the village and the inn is on the left.

Parking: There is a spacious car park at the rear of the pub.

Length of the walk: 2¾ miles. Map: OS Landranger 118 Stoke-on-Trent and Macclesfield (inn GR 933523).

Glorious views of the wooded Churnet valley unfold on this short walk, which crosses Stanley Pool, a man-made expanse of water popular with fishermen and boating enthusiasts.

The Walk

From the inn turn left and walk along the road for a short distance until you see a gap in the right-hand boundary. Head diagonally across a pasture and cross into the next field. There are very good views to the south, across spectacular, semi-wooded countryside. Turn immediately left and skirt the field, keeping the stone wall on your left. At a footpath sign, cross into the field on your left and continue in the same direction, with the wall now on your right. Over to your left are distant glimpses of the southern foothills of the Peak District and the Staffordshire Moorlands.

Make for the field corner and then continue ahead, with trees and hedgerow on your immediate left. Go down to the bottom corner of the field, pass through a gap in the hedge and head straight across

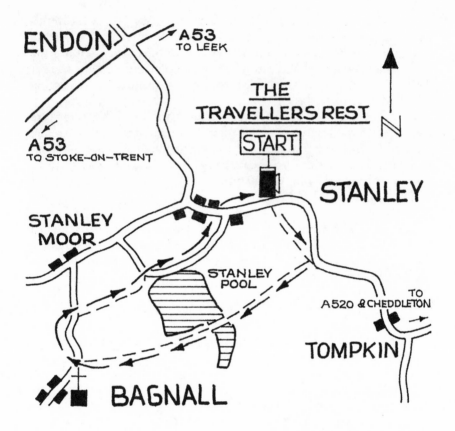

the next field towards a stile and two footbridges. Ignore a
signposted path to your left; instead, follow the path along the
right-hand edge of the woodland, with views across open
countryside on the right. Keep along the woodland edge and head
down through the trees. Further on, you come to Stanley Pool,
where you follow the raised path or causeway across the reservoir.
Stanley Pool was created as a feeder for the Caldon Canal and
achieved some notoriety in the late 1920s when it flooded and
swamped the Endon valley

Continue to a stile and a fork of paths. Disregard the right of way
running off half-left and take the path straight up the field. There are
good views across to Stanley Pool at this point of the walk, while
ahead of you are the houses of Bagnall. Pass through a gap in the

field boundary and continue to a stile in the top wall. Follow the field edge, with a hedgerow on the right, and look for a gap ahead by some bungalows. Make for the road and turn right, following it for about ½ mile, with impressive views down towards Cheddleton and Denford. The lovely Churnet valley dominates the scene and down below in the foreground is the outline of Stanley Pool.

Pass a bungalow called Fairhaven and a turning for the Sailing Centre car park. Bear right by Pool Bungalow and follow the signposted track round to the left and behind a line of houses. When the track ends, continue along a path, with a stone wall on the right, and on the higher ground there are splendid views of Stanley Pool and its colourful sailing boats. Follow the path over rough grassland, cross a boundary wall and drop down to a track at the northern end of the reservoir. Follow the track away from the pool and soon you will reach the road, with the dam hard by you on the right. Turn right, cross the little stone road bridge over the pretty feeder stream and follow the lane up into Stanley. At the next junction turn right and return to the inn.

Places of interest nearby
Cheddleton Flint Mill dates from the latter half of the 18th century and has been fully restored in recent years. Two undershot wheels were turned by the millrace in order to grind flint powder, which was then transported by barge to the Potteries where it became an important ingredient in the production of ceramics. The mill is open to the public at certain times and is widely acknowledged as one of the county's best-known and most popular tourist attractions. Telephone: 01782 502907. *Cheddleton Railway Centre* is based at an old Victorian country station, complete with signal box and mainline locomotives. There are steam rides on summer Sundays, as well as many other special events taking place. The site includes a small relics museum, refreshment room and souvenir shop. Telephone: 01538 360522.

4 Wetton
Ye Olde Royal Oak

Wetton is one of Staffordshire's loneliest villages, not that its residents mind that. Its setting high in the limestone hills of the southern Peak District makes it a perfect place in which to live. Not surprisingly, it is also very popular with tourists and walkers, particularly in the summer months.

Ye Olde Royal Oak, the only hostelry in the village, is a classic 300-year-old inn with white stone walls and shutters and a cosy, inviting atmosphere inside. Among the many charming features is a surviving relic from long ago: in a corner of the bar is a hatch for serving sheep and cattle drovers who were made to stand outside as they were considered too smelly to be allowed in the pub! Ye Olde Royal Oak is famous for being the home of the world toe wrestling championships, an event which has featured prominently in the press and on national television.

Food is served every day and includes several starters, with soup of the day being a popular choice in winter. Among the main courses are cheeseburger, chicken, ham with egg, lasagne, home-made mince and onion pie, plaice, scampi, trout, sausages and omelettes. There are vegetarian meals, various sandwiches, jacket potatoes, salads and ploughman's lunches. Children's meals are also available and there is a selection of sweets and a traditional Sunday roast. The pub features several beers on handpump – Theakston XB and Ruddles County among them. For those who drink lager, there is Stella Artois, Carlsberg and Heineken and Guinness, Olde English and Addlestones draught ciders are also available.

Ye Olde Royal Oak offers accommodation in four en suite bedrooms and there is also a sun lounge and an overflow garden bar, both of which overlook the beer garden at the rear of the inn. No dogs please. The pub is open from 12 noon to 2.30 pm and 7 pm to 11 pm in winter, 11.30 am to 3 pm and 6.30 pm to 11 pm in summer on Monday to Saturday, and from 12 noon to 3 pm and 7 pm to 10.30 pm on Sunday. Food is served from 12 noon to 2 pm and 6.30 pm to 9 pm (7 pm in winter).

Telephone: 01335 310287.

How to get there: From Leek or Ashbourne follow the A523 and join the B5053 north towards Buxton. Pass through the village of Onecote and then bear right, signposted Grindon. Drive through the village, follow narrow lanes and cross the river Manifold. Take the next left for Wetton and the public car park is on the left.To reach the pub, walk along the road and turn left at the junction to find the inn on your left.

Parking: As the pub gets very busy at certain times, the landlord requests that people use the public car park on the edge of the village.

Length of the walk: 3¼ miles. Map: OS Landranger 119 Buxton, Matlock and Dove Dale (inn GR 108554).

This is a lovely walk through the beautiful Manifold valley. The views over rolling limestone country are stunning, especially from the entrance to Thor's Cave. Beyond the cave, the walk follows a stretch of the Manifold Way beside the meandering river. The willow warbler can be heard at certain times and the purple orchid adds a touch of colour in summer.

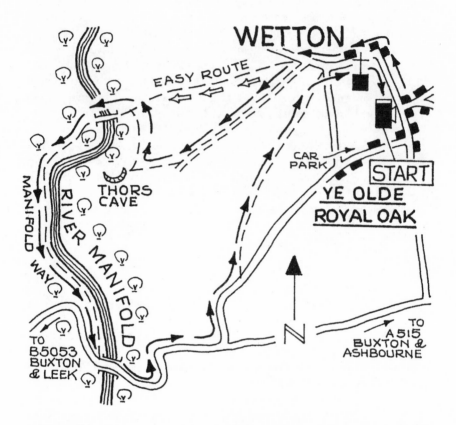

The Walk

From the pub turn left and follow the village street round to the left. Pass the 19th- century church and several footpath signs on the left and continue along the street between limestone cottages. Veer right at the next road junction and now you are faced with a choice. To visit Thor's Cave take the signposted concessionary track and follow it across the fields. Further on, you join a path, slippery at times, which takes you to the cave entrance at the top of some steps.

From here the views are tremendous. The cave takes its name from Thor, Norse God of thunder, and human remains were once unearthed here. A local schoolteacher, Samuel Carrington, explored the cave during the last century and discovered flint arrowheads, bone combs, bronze bracelets and brooches and a

Roman coin. I clambered up to the entrance, sometimes likened to the arched doorway of a Norman cathedral, but all was silent inside the dank and rather eerie chamber, apart the distant trickling of water. From the cave entrance, walk down to the bottom of the steps, taking care as you go, and bear left at the fork. Follow the path down through the trees and eventually you come down to a footbridge over the river Manifold. Cross over, look up to see Thor's Cave looming above you and then turn left to join the Manifold Way.

To avoid the cave, pass the concessionary track on the outskirts of Wetton and walk down the lane for a few yards until you reach a waymarked path on the left (Thor's Cave – ½ mile). Take the path and ahead of you are magnificent views of the Manifold valley, a majestic landscape of rolling green hills and limestone dales. Follow the path down the field, pass through a gap in the boundary and continue descending the slope towards some trees and bushes. Make for the bottom boundary and join a path running through the woodland. The path can be wet and very slippery in places. Pass a signposted path on the left, climbing steeply to Thor's Cave, and keep going through the trees.

Cross the Manifold river and then turn left to join Manifold Way. The track follows the route of the old Leek and Manifold Valley Light Railway, which ran for 30 years, between 1904 and 1934, and played a key role in the transportation of milk from this part of the Peak District to the Potteries. The lines were removed just before the Second World War and today the old trackbed is a very popular walking and cycle route. Follow the Manifold Way, keeping parallel to the river, which may, at times, be just a dry river-bed. In places the Manifold river disappears down what are known as 'swallet' holes in the limestone, so that above ground there is often no trace of the river. Keep to the route as it snakes through the valley and eventually you come to a parking area just before the road. Turn left at the road, cross a cattle-grid and go round to the left, then climb steeply round several bends to reach higher ground, affording beautiful views over the valley. Pass a footpath, go over a cattle-grid and take the next turning on the left.

Follow the lane, pass the village sign for Wetton then a footpath on the left and keep to the lane as it curves round to the right, looking out for a stile in the left boundary. Veer half-right across the field and make for an opening in the wall. Go straight across to a step-stile and waymarker in the next boundary, then diagonally left in the next field to the far corner and a choice of tracks. Take the concrete one on the left and keep to the left of some farm outbuildings. Cross a step-stile and continue on the track to the road. To visit the pub, turn left, then first right and head along the village street. To return to the car park, turn right and walk along to the junction, where you turn left to find the car park on your left.

Places of interest nearby
The Staffordshire Moorlands and *Southern Peak District* offer numerous beautiful walks; many of the old railway tracks make for very pleasant walking or cycling. *Dove Dale* is one of the region's most famous beauty spots. The towering rock formations and the tree-lined slopes are particularly attractive. However, try and avoid it on summer weekends when it becomes very crowded.

5 Betley
The Black Horse

Betley is one of north-west Staffordshire's most attractive villages, its wide main street lined with striking half-timbered houses and cottages. During the 13th century it became a borough with its local economy boosted somewhat by a weekly market; many buyers travelled here from neighbouring towns and villages and from adjoining counties. The Black Horse is one of Betley's oldest buildings, parts of it dating back to 1603.

Food is served every day – at lunchtime there is soup of the day, chef's traditional roast of the day, tender braised steak, lamb's liver and onions, cod steak, fresh grilled plaice, scampi, chicken Kiev, beefburger, steak and kidney pie and home-made lasagne. There are several vegetarian dishes, including cheese and broccoli bake and spinach and ricotta cannelloni, as well as a good range of sandwiches and toasties and a choice of jacket potatoes. A specials board is also available at lunchtime. The evening menu is very popular, featuring various starters, grills and speciality steaks, fresh fish and poultry dishes. Children have their own menu to choose from. For the beer drinker there is Marston's Pedigree and Banks's Bitter, plus a guest real ale on hand pump.

There is a beer garden at the rear of the inn, with a children's play area; dogs are permitted in the stable bar only. The Black Horse is open from 12 noon to 3 pm and 7 pm (6 pm in summer) to 11 pm Monday to Saturday and 12 noon to 3 pm and 7 pm to 10.30 pm on Sunday. Food is served from 12 noon to 2 pm and 7 pm to 9.30 pm (10 pm on Saturday). Please book if you require a table in the restaurant at the weekend.

Telephone: 01270 820166.

How to get there: Betley is located on the A531, roughly midway between Newcastle-under-Lyme and Nantwich. The inn is in the main street of the village.

Parking: There is plenty of room to park at the rear of the pub.

Length of the walk: 3 miles. Map: OS Landranger 118 Stoke-on-Trent and Macclesfield (inn GR 753486).

Some of Staffordshire's prettiest countryside can be seen on this pleasantly varied walk which follows field and woodland paths to the north-east of Betley.

The Walk
On leaving the pub turn right, cross the road and walk along to the junction with Church Lane. Bear left, then as the lane bends right to the 17th-century church, go straight on, passing a residential road (Ladygates) on the left and continue ahead along the 'no through road'. Follow it as it bends to the left and then down the slope between banks of trees and round to the right. Pass several bungalows and then ascend the slope.

At the top look for a footpath sign and a stile on the left. Veer diagonally right across the field, aiming just to the left of an oak tree. Cross the stile and descend the slope, heading obliquely right. Cross a footbridge at the bottom of the slope and look for a stile taking you into a patch of woodland. Follow the path through the trees to another stile in the top boundary. Cross the field diagonally, heading for the right-hand edge of a tongue of woodland. Make for a gate just to the right of the trees and then

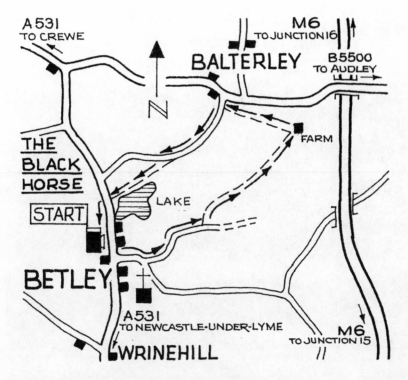

follow a grassy track with a fence on the right.

As you approach a farm, look for a waymarker and follow the path round the side of the outbuildings. Pass a sheep dip, go through a gate and join a drive which curves left in front of the farmhouse. Follow it through some pretty countryside to the road and turn left. Keep going along the lane and, in time, it curves to the right between hedgerows. Beyond the bend look for a path on the left, just as you reach some woodland. Go through the trees and head straight across a parking area to reach a stile.

Proceed across the tree-ringed field, keeping the road parallel on the right and soon a lake is glimpsed over on the left between the trees. Keep to the right of a marshy pond, pass a large house overlooking the lake and continue towards the buildings of Betley. Drop down to the bottom left-hand corner of the field and look for a stile by a stone wall. Follow a path alongside a copse to the main road and turn left. Pass the Betley village sign and walk back along the main street to the inn.

Etruria, Stoke-on-Trent
The China Garden

Etruria lies at the heart of the Potteries and it was here in 1766 that Josiah Wedgwood established his world famous factory. The 'Father of the Pottery Industry' built an entire village for his employees and gave it an Italian name because he believed, mistakenly, that a renowned classical vase he greatly admired was Etruscan. The pottery complex moved to nearby Barlaston at the beginning of the Second World War and the cheerless industrial landscape at Etruria has long gone, transformed beyond recognition during the last few years as part of an award-winning land reclamation scheme. The site was the venue for the famous National Garden Festival of 1986 and today the Festival Park offers a variety of things to see and do. Parkland and picnic areas, snooker, superbowl, a 10-screen cinema and a dry ski centre are among the attractions.

The China Garden was built in 1985 to coincide with the National Garden Festival and its position alongside the Trent and Mersey Canal makes it a popular choice for many families. This modern pub is very spacious and inside there is a lounge, family room, games area and restaurant. A glance at the menu reveals a variety of dishes – there is cream of tomato soup, stockpot soup, melon, prawn cocktail and crispy-fried mushrooms among the starters. Main courses include steaks, fish and chicken dishes, salads and vegetarian meals. Double jacket potatoes and omelettes are also featured. The China Garden offers a children's menu and a traditional Sunday roast. A range of ales is available, including Parsons Porter and Bass; there are several lagers – Tennent's Pilsner, Carling Black Label, Premier – and Caffrey's Bitter and Dry Blackthorn cider are also on offer.

Tables and benches enable you to sit outside and enjoy the activity on the water, as adjoining the pub is a marina crowded with colourful narrow boats. No dogs please. The China Garden is open from 12 noon to 2.30 pm and 5.30 pm to 11 pm Monday to Friday and all day on Saturday and Sunday. Food is served from 12 noon to 2 pm and 5.30 pm to 10.30 pm.

Telephone: 01782 260199.

How to get there: Follow the A500 and turn off at the signs for the Festival Park. Bear left (signposted marina and entertainment) and the pub will be found on the left.

Parking: There is plenty of room to park at the inn.

Length of the walk: 4 miles. Map: OS Landranger 118 Stoke-on-Trent and Macclesfield (inn GR 868474). There are several visitor street maps and guides for Hanley and Etruria available from the Tourist Information Centre in Quadrant Road, Hanley. Telephone: 01782 284600.

'The Potteries – firing the imagination' proclaims the advertising slogan. Few would disagree with that. Certainly this town trail around Hanley and Etruria reveals something new and unexpected at every turn, discovering the area's fascinating industrial and architectural heritage.

The Walk
From the front of the inn go down to the towpath of the Trent and Mersey Canal and turn left. Cross the little swingbridge, keep the

marina on the left and continue beside the waterway. The canal was the inspiration of Josiah Wedgwood who commissioned the engineering genius James Brindley to construct 'The Grand Trunk' to enable kaolin clay and flint to be transported directly to his factory from other parts of the country. Go up to the dual carriageway, cross over and continue on the right-hand bank of the canal. The occasional long boat or cruiser can be seen on this stretch of the waterway. On the right is a fascinating industrial landscape; factory chimneys and church spires can be seen stretching to the horizon. Pass the junction of the Trent and Mersey Canal and the Caldon Canal, which was originally built to carry minerals from the Peak District to the Potteries and is now a very popular leisure-based inland waterway.

Keep to the towpath, passing the Etruria maintenance yard on the left. Walk beside the next lock and, on the opposite side of the canal, you can see the Etruscan Bone and Flint Mill, part of the Etruria Industrial Museum. The steam-powered mill was built in 1857 to grind materials, including bone and flint, for the agricultural and pottery industries. Much of its original machinery has been restored and visitors to the site can see one of the oldest steam engines still in working order. You can also see the Princess in steam on certain days. Cross the bridge and after visiting the museum, return to the towpath and follow it to Twyford Lock. Pass under the very low road bridge – tall people will be forced to stoop here!

A cemetery and the buildings of Hanley can be seen on the opposite bank. On the right are several bottle-shaped brick ovens, which are a familiar sight in this part of Staffordshire, recalling the great era of the Potteries. Sadly, many of the ovens have disappeared over the years. Continue along the towpath and a railway line is visible on the right now. Pass an iron milepost at the next lock and go under the bridge. Just beyond it, turn right at a gap in the fence and follow the path along to the footbridge over the railway. Cross over and pass some lock-up garages, with the cemetery now on your left. Continue straight on, with the iron railings of the fence on your immediate left.

At the main road junction, go across into Avenue Road and follow it to the mini-roundabout. Cross over and enter Hanley Park, following the path as it curves to the right, with an expansive lake on your right. Hanley Park is a splendid example of urban public gardens, for with its network of paths, bandstand, lake and tennis courts, it has the stamp of a classic town park. Just before reaching the hard tennis courts, turn sharp left and follow the path to some steps, and go up them to a bandstand. Make for another flight of steps and turn left in front of a large building.

Follow the path and soon it begins to curve to the right. Pass a children's play area, bear left at a fork and walk along to the road where you turn right. Pass Cooper Street and at the next junction, by St Mark's church, bear right and follow the main road. The Victoria Hotel is seen ahead; beyond it you come to a roundabout. Turn right and walk along the dual carriageway as far as the pedestrian crossing. Cross over into Cannon Street, then proceed straight on at the next junction and go up several flights of steps,

Etruria Industrial Museum (courtesy of Stoke-on-Trent C.C., Tourism Division).

before turning left to reach the entrance to the City Museum and Art Gallery. Open daily, it contains the world's largest collection of Staffordshire ceramics, as well as various exhibitions and a celebration of 300 years of fashion and style – among other attractions. The museum also includes the Mark XVI Spitfire, designed by Reginald Mitchell who was a local man.

On leaving the museum, turn left and walk along Bethesda Street and then turn right into Albion Street. Hanley, birthplace of Arnold Bennett who immortalised the Potteries in his classic stories of the Five Towns, is one of six separate towns that collectively make up Stoke-on-Trent. Hanley is the main shopping centre and therefore one of the busiest of the towns. Pass the council offices and note the war memorial. Bear left by C&A into Stafford Street and walk along to the award-winning Potteries Shopping Centre and factory shop complex. On leaving the centre, cross Stafford Street into Piccadilly and then bear right into Brunswick Street. Go down to the junction and straight across into Clough Street. Follow it all the way to the next junction and then cross over into Etruria Park. Follow the path diagonally through the park, keep to the left of the drinking fountain and head down to a gate. Turn left and walk along the road until you reach the canal bridge. Cross the road, join the towpath and return to the pub.

Places of interest nearby
The *Etruria Industrial Museum* is open all year from Wednesday to Sunday, except Christmas and New Year. Telephone: 01782 287557. The *Gladstone Pottery Museum* at Longton includes some original bottle ovens and various workshops where craftsmen can be seen making and decorating pottery. Telephone: 01782 319232. Stoke-on-Trent is famous for its range of factory shops which include everything from fine china dinner services, table and cookware, to mugs, jugs and tiles. Further details are included in the 'China Experience' leaflet available from the Tourist Information Centre.

7 Foxt
The Fox and Goose

Foxt is a quiet village perched 800 feet above the richly wooded Churnet valley. Close by are vivid reminders of the days when this area echoed to the sound of industry. The copper works at Froghall and the quarries at Cauldon Low have long gone. Today, the scene has changed beyond recognition and many people now choose this place for its peaceful walks and scenic beauty.

The Fox and Goose, the only remaining pub in the village, dates back to the second half of the 19th century and for years was run as a Bass house until the company sold it. The inn still has the air of a traditional local, with a cosy fire, and many of the local characters who drink here will entertain you with colourful stories of life as it used to be in Foxt and the surrounding district.

The pub offers a range of snacks, salads and sandwiches – ham, beef and cheese are among the fillings available. For something more substantial, there is scampi, plaice, salmon and trout, as well as the locally renowned Fox and Goose pie and a choice of traditional roast meals – pork, beef, turkey or lamb. There are several lagers, including Carling Black Label and Carlsberg, Guinness and Dry Blackthorn cider, and the real ales on draught are Bass and a guest ale, such as Morland Old Speckled Hen, which is named after a distinctive, speckled MG car.

Outside the inn is a pleasant garden and children's play area. Dogs are also permitted, though not in the dining areas. The Fox and Goose is open every day, except Monday lunchtime, from 12 noon to 2.30 pm and 7 pm to 11 pm and 12 noon to 3 pm and 7 pm to 10.30 pm on Sunday. Food is available daily, except Sunday and Monday evening, from 12 noon to 2 pm and 7 pm to 10 pm. Larger groups are requested to book.

Telephone: 01538 266415.

How to get there: Follow the A52 between Stoke-on-Trent and Ashbourne. Head north at Froghall, following the signs for Froghall Wharf and Foxt. The inn is in the village centre.

Parking: There is a car park at the front of the inn.

Length of the walk: 2½ miles. Map: OS Landranger 119 Buxton, Matlock and Dove Dale (inn GR 035485).

This pretty walk drops down into the Churnet valley, passing through a nature reserve to reach historic Froghall Wharf at the terminus of the Caldon Canal. From here the route follows an old disused tramway before cutting through woodland and across fields to return to the hilltop village of Foxt.

The Walk
Leave the inn and take the road leading towards Froghall and the A52. Follow the lane as it twists and turns, affording very good views of the wooded valley. Pass a row of terraced houses on the left and then take the left turn immediately beyond them, following the sign for Froghall Wharf. Head down the grassy track to a gate and go straight on for a few yards in the next field, pass through a gateway and then descend the sometimes slippery bank, passing between trees and bushes.

Veer right at the bottom and cross a stile. Go over a stream and follow the woodland path through Harston Nature Reserve. Ash, elm, alder, hazel and oak are among the variety of trees to be found

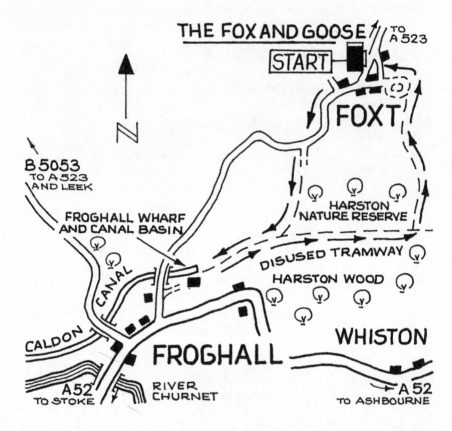

THE FOX AND GOOSE

TO A 523

START

FOXT

B 5053
TO A 523
AND LEEK

HARSTON
NATURE RESERVE

FROGHALL WHARF
AND CANAL BASIN

DISUSED TRAMWAY

HARSTON WOOD

CANAL

WHISTON

CALDON

FROGHALL

A 52
TO STOKE

RIVER
CHURNET

A 52
TO ASHBOURNE

within its boundaries. On reaching a junction of paths, turn left and go up some steps to the old tramway. To visit Froghall Wharf, turn right and follow the path along to the parking and picnic area. Originally, quarrying, mining and the transportation and burning of limestone were the chief industries here. The site, now a popular recreational area with visitors and walkers, has been transformed beyond recognition over the years, though there are still visible reminders of Froghall's industrial past, including several limekilns, disused tramways, the canal basin and the old wharf buildings, where refreshments are available in the summer months. Froghall Wharf came into being as a direct result of the cutting of the Caldon Canal in the late 18th century. Intended to act as a feeder to the Trent and Mersey Canal and to provide access to raw materials, the

Caldon Canal was built by James Brindley who became ill with pneumonia whilst surveying the canal terminus at Froghall and died a few days later. Work on completing the Caldon Canal was later taken over by John Rennie.

To continue the main walk, bear left, waymarked 'Froghall Wharf Walk'. Your route follows the former tramway, cutting between high banks and lines of trees. There were four tramways linking Froghall Wharf with the nearby Cauldon Low limestone quarries. With a little imagination, it is possible to picture the great wagons loaded with limestone, making their way along this track to Froghall Wharf where waiting barges would transport the materials to the rest of the country. In 1849 a cable railway replaced the trams. Continue through the cutting and on the right is the outline of Harston Rock. Various sandstone cliffs and outcrops are also visible along this stretch of the walk. Proceed on the tramway until you see a signposted path on the left, heading down some steps into the trees. Go down through the woodland and then up to a stile. Skirt a field, keeping to the left-hand edge and drop down to a footbridge over a brook.

Go straight across the next field to a stile and then through some trees to a second footbridge and climb another stile. Follow the path alongside a dry-stone wall and climb steeply to the field corner. Veer right and continue over the high ground, keeping the wall beside you on the left until you reach a squeeze-stile. Follow a track to a road, turn right, then right again to reach a junction. Bear left and the inn is on the right.

Place of interest nearby
The *Wildlife Sanctuary* at Kingsley, near Cheadle, offers visitors the opportunity to witness many species of birds and mammals from all over the world. The site also includes a visitor centre, gift shop and light refreshments. Telephone: 01538 754784.

8 Oakamoor
The Lord Nelson

Oakamoor's setting in the wooded Churnet valley is truly delightful. A guide to the Staffordshire Way describes it as being at 'the centre of perhaps the most varied and beautiful wooded area in the county'. The Lord Nelson is one of several public houses in Oakamoor. I first called here many years ago whilst walking the Staffordshire Way. Having checked into the nearby youth hostel for the night, my next priority was to investigate the local hostelries. As I know from personal experience, trekking Britain's long distance footpaths can be a thirsty business!

The Lord Nelson dates back to the 18th century and in its time has been a tearoom, a doctor's surgery and even a casualty unit for those people who had been involved in industrial accidents at the nearby copper works. The pub is very popular with walkers and you can even bring your own food with you, if that is your preference. If you book in advance, the landlord will easily accommodate groups of ramblers and arrange food to suit most tastes. Soup of the day and various sandwiches are perennial favourites with walkers, though for something more substantial you could choose scampi, plaice, steak and ale casserole, chicken and mushroom pie, chilli con carne, lasagne, or chicken or lamb provençal. There is also a children's menu, a play area in the garden and a barn where barbecues take place in summer. Worthington Best Bitter and Bass, alongside a guest beer, are the real ales served on hand pump. For the lager drinker, there is Carling Black Label and Tennent's Extra and Guinness is available for those who prefer stout. Woodpecker and Scrumpy Jack cider are also served on draught.

The pub, which also offers accommodation and a 22-seater restaurant, is open from 12 noon to 3 pm and 7 pm to 11 pm (10.30 pm on Sunday). Food is served daily, except Thursday, from 12 noon to 2 pm and 7.30 pm to 9 pm. The bar sometimes stays open all day, depending on the level of customers. It is advisable to book for the restaurant, especially at weekends and in the summer. Well behaved dogs are allowed inside the pub.

Telephone: 01538 702242.

How to get there: Oakamoor lies on the B5417, midway between Cheadle and the A52. Turn off at the Cricketers Arms and the inn is a short distance along the road.

Parking: There is a car park at the side of the pub.

Length of the walk: 3½ miles. Map: OS Landranger 119 Buxton, Matlock and Dove Dale (inn GR 054451).

The first half of this scenic walk in the Churnet valley follows a disused railway line, now a popular woodland trail, running alongside the river. The route then follows a stretch of the Staffordshire Way through Ousal Dale before returning to Oakamoor. A variety of trees, including many conifers and hardwoods, can be seen on the route.

The Walk

From the pub walk down the street, passing the village hall and the war memorial. Turn right at the main road and then cross over to join a path, signposted Churnet valley. After a few yards, the path bends round to the right and cuts between silver birch trees,

affording a pretty view of the four-arched stone road bridge on the right. Head straight across the meadow, keeping the Churnet on the right, and further on you pass a footbridge. Rowan, field maple and ornamental willow are among the trees you are likely to spot in the Churnet valley, with alders growing on the river bank.

Remain on the left bank, following the riverside path to a junction with another track. Bear left here and very shortly you will reach the platform of an old dilapidated railway station on the long abandoned Churnet Line, which enabled people to travel from nearby Alton to work at Oakamoor and neighbouring Froghall. Follow the route of the disused line, walking along the old trackbed between lines of trees. On your right a curtain of woodland rises up to the skyline, beyond the expanse of a sports field, and the river is occasionally visible to your right. Proceed along this path, the scene hardly changing at all for over a mile.

About 50 yards before you reach the next bridge, with a wall of sandstone on the left, turn left to cross a footbridge. Follow the path up to the bridge, turn right and cross the former railway line and the river. Ahead of you now is a popular inn, the Rambler's Retreat. Cross the road and keep to the right of the pub, following the sign for the smelting mill. Walk along the track and soon you pass a large fish pond and the site of the old mill, originally used for smelting lead ore from Ecton. By the late 18th century it had become a corn grinding mill where a 20 foot high breast water wheel drove three pairs of stones.

Follow the route of the Staffordshire Way, continuing along the track with the pond on your left. Pass to the right of a cottage and follow the track signposted 'The Ranger'. Rabbits and hares may be seen on this stretch of the walk through Ousal Dale. Keep going as the track climbs between banks of bracken and lines of beech and fir trees. Eventually you come up to a junction; turn left and as the path curves round to the left after several yards, go straight on and follow the rock-strewn path up to a track. On the left is the entrance to a youth hostel. Turn right and follow the Staffordshire Way sign for a few yards, then bear right before a cattle-grid.

Go up the bank, cross a track and follow a walled path, which curves round to the right, with glimpses of the lovely Churnet valley, often called the 'Staffordshire Rhineland', on this stretch of the walk. Look for a gate on the left and continue for a short distance until you are level with a white cottage. Turn left and drop down steeply through the dense woodland to reach a forest track. Turn left and follow it for about 20 yards, then veer half-right and continue descending between the trees. The path can be wet and slippery at times, particularly in winter.

Turn left at the road and follow it to the next junction. Bear right and walk along to a turning for the old station and then, beyond it, a picnic and parking area. It was on this site in the mid-19th century that a copper works, established by Thomas Bolton in 1797, produced the copper wire for the first successful transatlantic cable linking Europe with America. Information panels in the car park illustrate Oakamoor's industrial heritage. You can return to the inn by turning right here and then retracing your steps across the meadows and through the trees of the Churnet valley, or, if you

Ramblers at Oakamoor.

prefer, you can continue along the road to Oakamoor. At the junction with the B5417 turn right, cross the river and then bear left for the inn.

Places of interest nearby
Alton Towers, Britain's most popular leisure attraction and theme park, is famous for its outstanding rides. There are also extensive gardens and woodlands to explore, and numerous other attractions to keep the family occupied for the entire day. Telephone: 01538 702200.

9 Swynnerton
The Fitzherbert Arms

Swynnerton is the quintessential English village. Its imposing 18th-century Hall, cricket ground and picturesque thatched cottages lend an air of dignified calm in a modern bustling world. Some sources suggest that Swynnerton was the inspiration for Longfellow's famous poem 'Under the Spreading Chestnut Tree'. There are few clues but a chestnut tree near the Fitzherbert Arms might have helped to give him the idea. The Fitzherbert Arms is owned by Lord Stafford, a member of the Fitzherbert family, who lives at the nearby Hall. One of his ancestors, Maria Fitzherbert, married the Prince of Wales, who later became George IV. However, the marriage was never fully recognised as Maria was a catholic.

With its beamed ceilings and various antiquities, the inn has a warm and welcoming atmosphere. There are black and white photographs showing the building as it used to be, and its Oak Room Restaurant has a fine reputation for food (booking essential). The pub offers a good selection of 'light bites' – including garlic mushrooms, chicken wings, toasted BLT, steak bap, smoked mackerel pâté, soup and a good range of sandwiches. Starters include prawn cocktail, tiger prawns, chicken liver pâté, deep-fried Camembert and an Indian savoury selection. Salmon steak, breaded scampi and Rob Roy trout are among the fish dishes and Cumberland sausages, beef curry and liver and bacon casserole are firm favourites. There is also a popular choice of grills, including various steaks, and a selection of home-made pies. Among the Fitzherbert Arms specialities are orange and cranberry duck, lemon and lime chicken, vegetable curry and garlic chicken. The inn also has a good choice of exotic puddings. Bass, Worthington Best Bitter and Gibbs Mew Salisbury Bitter are among the real ales on hand pump; there is also a guest beer. Carling Black Label and Caffrey's Irish Ale are available too.

The Fitzherbert Arms is open from 11.45 am to 2.30 pm and 6.45 pm to 11 pm Monday and Saturday and from 12 noon to 3 pm and 7 pm to 10.30 pm on Sunday. Food is served until 2.15 pm from Monday to Saturday and until 2.30 pm on Sunday. In the evenings last orders are at 9.30 pm from Sunday to Thursday and 10 pm on Friday and Saturday. Dogs are restricted to the public bar.

Telephone: 01782 796542.

How to get there: The easiest way to approach Swynnerton is from the A51. Head towards Crewe and Nantwich, cross the M6 and then follow the signs for Swynnerton. The inn is on the main road, in the village centre.

Parking: There is a spacious car park at the pub.

Length of the walk: 3½ miles. Map: OS Landranger 127 Stafford and Telford (inn GR 852356).

There are fine views on this walk, particularly on the outward leg as you look towards the spectacular wooded country around the Staffordshire/Cheshire border. The last mile or so of the circuit is within the boundaries of Swynnerton Park, offering very pleasant parkland scenery.

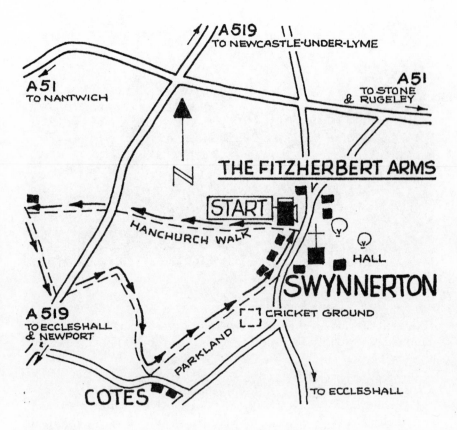

The Walk

From the front door of the inn turn right for a few yards, then right again into Early Lane and follow the tarmac lane with a wall on the left. Pass a wooden signpost for 'Hanchurch Walk' and continue to the edge of the village. The route coincides for some time with a signposted walk to the village of Hanchurch, which lies just to the west of the M6. At the end of the lane, continue ahead on a clear path between hedgerows. There are good views across a striking, rural landscape towards neighbouring Cheshire and Shropshire. Eventually, descend to a junction with several tracks and take the track ahead, signposted 'Hanchurch Walk', keeping a hedgerow on the right. Cross a field boundary and bear immediately left at the next sign for Hanchurch, then walk along a grassy track with a

Swynnerton Hall.

hedge on the left. In the field corner continue ahead, with the field boundary now on your immediate right and power lines over on the left.

Make for a gap in the hedgerow and shortly reach the A519. Cross over and continue on the 'Hanchurch Walk', passing under the power lines. Keep to the left-hand edge of the field and eventually a cottage comes into view up ahead. Head for the field corner, draw level with the cottage and turn left at a junction, leaving the route of the 'Hanchurch Walk'. Follow the path through the trees, pass a path on the right and at this point enjoy a lovely view over wooded parkland near Cranberry. Continue between margins of bracken, cursed by many farmers and landowners because it is so prolific and difficult to destroy. Pass through a gate and here there are good views over a wide, regal landscape dotted with trees and criss-crossed by hedgerows. Follow a rough track, keeping the hedgerow on the right and eventually reach a stile in the field corner. Go out to the road (A519), cross over to another stile, then follow the right-hand boundary of a field and make for a stile up ahead in the corner. There are some larch trees on the right here.

Cross the stile to join a wooded path and turn right, passing beneath the branches of some beech trees and beside a pond enclosed by light woodland. On the right are various industrial units, visible beyond the fence. Follow the path as it cuts across a picturesque landscape and, further on, it joins a wider track which is muddy in places. On reaching the road, continue ahead for about 10 yards until you see a footpath on the left. Take this path and cross a small paddock to another stile, then head straight across the next field, passing under some pylons. Make for a stile ahead and cut through some light woodland, following the path as it veers left through the trees.

Soon you come to another stile; cross over and walk ahead across Swynnerton Park. Pass a marsh pool and head towards some trees in the distance. Gradually the houses of Swynnerton edge into view up ahead. Cross a stile in the next boundary and pass alongside Swynnerton Park Cricket Club, founded in 1892. Keep to the left of the drive leading to the club and make for a stile up ahead. Cross the road and go straight ahead along a path cutting through a housing estate to join the road at the top of the slope and proceed straight ahead. Pass Frobisher Drive, Swynnerton's Anglican Church of St Mary and the Gothic-style Catholic church, which was built for the Fitzherbert family, and very soon you are back at the inn.

Places of interest nearby
Mill Meece Pumping Station includes the famous 'Gentle Giants' – working steam engines that were originally built to provide drinking water to the Potteries. The site has working displays of water processing, a range of short videos and a souvenir shop. From time to time, there are steam spectaculars, fairground organs and craft fairs. Telephone: 01270 873683.

⑩ Milwich
The Green Man

Milwich is one of the most attractive villages in this part of Staffordshire. It is said that the church contains the oldest bell in the county, dating back to the early 15th century and re-hung in 1977. The Green Man, the only pub in Milwich, is thought to have been built sometime around the 16th century, becoming a public house in 1775, and records indicate it has always been known as the Green Man. Throughout the 19th century, the inn was run by members of the Fairbanks family. The image of the pub has not changed that much during its lifetime. It has always been a traditional village pub, popular with local drinkers, and these days it is frequented more and more by groups of ramblers who are keen to sample a little liquid refreshment and local fare after spending a few hours in the surrounding countryside.

Toasted sandwiches and a bowl of soup are favourite choices, especially on a cold winter's day. However, there are other dishes to choose from, such as lasagne, fish bake, steak and kidney pie, curry, chilli con carne and freshly-cut sandwiches. There are also one or two vegetarian meals on the menu. Small groups who would prefer individually prepared food not generally found on the menu can usually be accommodated, though only by prior arrangement. Worthington Best Bitter is the regular cask conditioned ale pulled from the hand pump, and there is usually a choice of two popular guest beers. Carling Black Label and Tennent's Extra are also available, as are Scrumpy Jack cider and Murphy's stout.

The Green Man is open from 12 noon to 2 pm Monday to Thursday, 12 noon to 2.30 pm on Friday and 12 noon to 11 pm on Saturday. Evening hours are from 5 pm to 11 pm Monday to Friday. Sunday hours are from 12 noon to 3 pm and 7 pm to 10.30 pm. Food is served Wednesday to Sunday lunchtimes only from 12 noon to 2 pm. Larger parties are requested to book. Well behaved dogs are permitted in the bar and outside in the beer garden.

Telephone: 01889 505310.

How to get there: Milwich is on the B5027 Stone to Uttoxeter road. The Green Man is in the village centre, at the junction with the road to Sandon and the A51.

Parking: The inn has its own car park.

Length of the walk: 2¾ miles. Map: OS Landranger 127 Stafford and Telford (inn GR 973323).

Some of Staffordshire's prettiest countryside is explored on this delightful walk; a rich landscape of rolling hills, woodland and meandering streams.

The Walk
From the inn turn left towards Sandon and cross the road bridge over the stream. As the road begins to climb between the trees, look for a signposted footpath on the left leading to All Saints church and cross several stiles before entering the churchyard. Pass a seat to commemorate 850 years of Milwich church and take the path alongside the main door. Methodists came here to worship in 1982 after their chapel at nearby Garshall Green was closed. The history of All Saints is recorded at the entrance.

Continue to the churchyard's southern boundary, keeping a hedge on your right, and go through a kissing-gate into the

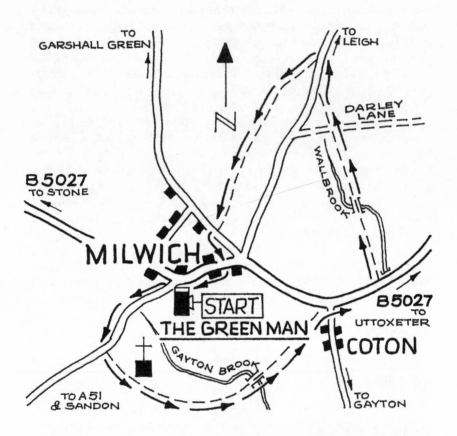

adjoining the field. Avoid the path heading t right down the slope
and go straight ahead across the field. Keep going until you see a
stile in the left boundary. Cross the stile, bear right and keep
alongside a pleasant stream, Gayton Brook, and a fence on your left
until you reach another stile. Cross a footbridge spanning the
brook and then go straight ahead for about 70 yards. Look for a
stile in the right-hand boundary, cross into the adjacent field, then
bear left and head up the grassy slope.

Pass a stile on the left and then veer slightly right to a stile by a
galvanized gate. Head towards some farm buildings, cross a drive
and then cut across the grass to another stile which takes you out to
the road. Turn right and follow the road round the left-hand bend,
passing an inn called the Wheatsheaf. The pub is attached to the

farm – unusual in the late 20th century. Walk past several houses and continue as the road curves left. Look for a stile beside a gate in the left-hand boundary and follow the field path alongside the Wall Brook, skirting a line of trees and bushes. Continue to the far corner, cross a stile and keep going along the edge of the next field until you reach a footbridge spanning the brook. Cross over and then bear immediately left. Follow the path between the stream and fence to the next stile and then go straight ahead in the next field, keeping the ditch on your left. About 70 yards before you reach the next boundary, veer half-left over the ditch and make for a stile in the field corner. Cross Darley Lane, a lovely undiscovered bridleway, and climb the stile opposite. Veer half-left through a gap in the trees and then head straight up the field to the stile in the top boundary.

Turn right for a few steps along the road, then bear left over a stile. Veer left in the field and make for another stile, with delightful vistas of distant wooded vales and crumpled green valleys ahead of you. Follow the clear path across a number of field boundaries, heading towards the buildings of Milwich, eventually reaching a stile and the road, opposite a row of houses. Turn left, walk along to the junction, then bear right and pass a very picturesque, timber-framed thatched cottage inlaid with herringbone brickwork. Continue along the village street and soon the Green Man looms into view. The B5027 is a former turnpike road and opposite the pub is a surviving tollhouse.

Place of interest nearby
The town of *Stone* expanded with the coming of the Trent & Mersey Canal and today it is still closely associated with this famous waterway. A stroll along the canal and a tour of the town reveal much of Stone's fascinating past.

11 Sandon
The Dog & Doublet

Sandon grew up around the nearby park, but its gradual expansion and the coming of the A51 led to a new community being established on the main road. The Dog & Doublet, just off the A51, is very popular with walkers. Several dozen ramblers were setting off from the pub car park when I arrived there one morning. The inn, which is also a hotel, was originally a staging post in the days when what is now the A51 was no more than a rough track. Coaches would stop here overnight and the remains of the old stables can be seen at the back.

Food is served every day throughout the year and as well as various starters, salads, vegetarian meals and sandwiches, there is a good choice of main courses – plaice, haddock, scampi, seafood platter, steaks, grills, gammon with egg or pineapple, chicken Kiev and a selection of home-made specials among them. Scampi and sausage, egg and chips are included in the children's menu and on Sunday there is a traditional roast lunch. Bass and Worthington Best Bitter are the beers served on hand pump. There is also a choice of several lagers, including Carling Black Label and Tennent's, and Beamish stout and Caffrey's Irish Ale are also available.

The Dog & Doublet offers overnight accommodation in 4 double rooms, a function room, skittle alley and non-smoking dining room, for which it is advisable to book. Dogs are restricted to the beer garden. The inn, which also serves morning coffee, is open from 11.30 am to 3 pm and 6 pm to 11 pm Monday to Friday, 11.30 am to 11 pm on Saturday and 12 noon to 10.30 pm on Sunday. During the summer the pub is open all day throughout the week. Food is served from 12 noon to 2.30 pm and 6 pm to 9.30 pm.

Telephone: 01889 508331.

How to get there: Follow the A51 between Rugeley and Stone and join the B5066 at Sandon. The Dog & Doublet will be found immediately on the left.

Parking: There is plenty of room to park at the inn.

Length of the walk: 2¼ miles. Map: OS Landranger 127 Stafford and Telford (inn GR 947293).

This short walk explores Sandon Park, visiting the prominent, hilltop church of All Saints before cutting across open countryside back to Sandon. The route offers spectacular views across the Trent valley.

The Walk
From the front door of the pub turn right and straight away you will see the distinctive Sandon war memorial located at the junction with the A51. Sandon lies in the shadow of Sandon Park and one of the estate's imposing entrances can be seen on the far side of the main road. The present Sandon Hall, designed in the Jacobean style, was built in 1852 for the 2nd Earl of Harrowby and within the extensive parkland are monuments to two famous statesmen. One is a 75 foot column in memory of William Pitt and erected by the first Earl of Harrowby, Foreign Secretary during Pitt's administration. The other is a Gothic shrine dedicated to Spencer Perceval, a Tory Prime Minister, who was assassinated in 1812 by an aggrieved merchant in the lobby of the House of Commons.

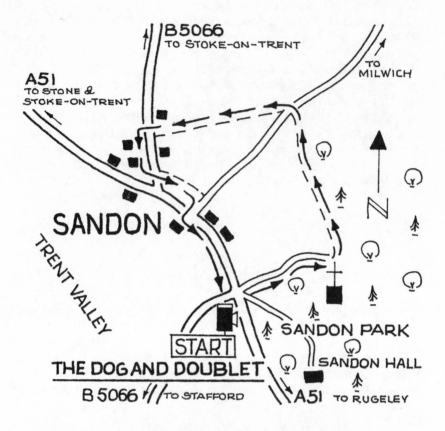

Cross the main road and take the lane (no through road) in front of you, keeping the gate into Sandon Park on your right. Pass a sign for Thomas Cottage and some farm outbuildings, then bear right at the next junction and follow the lane between fences, trees and hedgerows, affording good views over Sandon Park. Pass a house on the right and continue to where the lane curves left. At this point you have a choice of routes to the church. A footpath on the right crosses the field to the churchyard; alternatively, you could continue along the sunken lane, following it round to the right and along to a white gate leading into the churchyard. From here there are delightful views over the Trent valley. The ancient Church of All Saints contains several monuments to the Erdeswicke family whose manor once stood on the site of what is now Sandon Park.

The churchyard, which is bounded on one side by a line of yew trees, includes the tombstones of several 18th-century vicars. Many of the comments in the visitor book suggest that most people who call here cannot fail to be impressed by the church's peaceful parkland setting.

Emerging from the churchyard, go straight ahead across the turf. On the right a vast sweep of Sandon Park stretches to the horizon; a majestic landscape of rolling parkland dotted with trees. Ahead of you now is a wooded hummock; veer a little to the left of it and over to the left are glimpses of the Trent valley. Continue across the slopes, keeping the crown of trees on the right and a field boundary fence eventually appears up ahead. Make for a gate by some beech trees and then go diagonally across the next field, heading for the far corner. Look for a gate and emerge to the road.

Go straight over to a gate and then follow a grassy track between a hedge and fence. Pass under the boughs of some oak trees and beside lines of crops and make for the gate in the field corner. Pheasants may suddenly emerge from the undergrowth – so be warned! Cross the next field obliquely to a gateway in a line of trees, then head down the slope and look for the buildings of Sandon in the distance. Head for a gate in the bottom corner of the field and then ascend a grassy slope, keeping to the right of some farm buildings and barns up ahead. Cross two stiles in quick succession to reach the road. Turn left and walk down towards the A51, soon to reach a stretch of pavement. Turn left just before the 'give way' sign and follow a green lane lined with oak trees and hedgerows. At the next junction, opposite a footpath, bear right and walk along the road to the junction with the A51. Turn left and return to the inn.

Places of interest nearby
Stafford includes many attractions and a stroll around the town centre reveals many historic buildings and places of interest. The Ancient High House, Tixall Gatehouse, Broad Eye Windmill and Chetwynd House are all worth a visit, as is Stafford Castle. For more details, telephone the Tourist Information Centre: 01785 240204.

12 High Offley
The Anchor

High Offley is a quiet, mid-Staffordshire village hidden in remote farming country bisected by the Shropshire Union Canal. In common with many other villages in the area, High Offley once belonged to the Bishop of Lichfield who had a summer residence at Eccleshall.

The Anchor lies nearly a mile from the centre of High Offley, on the south bank of the canal. Surrounded by open countryside and with few other buildings nearby, it is an unusually isolated, completely unspoilt and genuine country inn harking back to a bygone age when pubs were simple alehouses with few of today's comforts and attractions. With its original furnishings, including settles and tables, it has, as a hostelry, a reputation for being one of Staffordshire's timeless gems. The Anchor has been in the same family for over a century. One of its most famous landladies was the late Mrs Pascal who ran the pub for more than 60 years and was still serving behind the bar in her late eighties. Originally, this 19th-century pub was frequented by bargees and canal workers, though nowadays its customers are mainly leisure-based – walkers, caravanners, boating enthusiasts and the like.

A limited snack menu is available. There are sandwiches and toasted sandwiches, with various fillings such as salmon, cheese and ham. Westons cider is a noted speciality here, with about a dozen different ones to choose from, such as pear, vintage, sweet and extra dry – among others. The popular beer Wadworth 6X is served on hand pump throughout the year and Marston's Pedigree is also available during the summer. There is also bottled lager and Guinness.

Outside are various tables and benches where in summer you can relax and enjoy the view of the canal. Dogs are welcome. Adjacent to the inn is a campsite with a gift shop which is open at weekends. The Anchor is open during the summer months from 11 am to 3 pm and 6 pm to 11 pm Monday to Saturday and 12 noon to 3 pm and 7 pm to 10.30 pm on Sunday. In winter the inn is open on Friday evening from 7 pm to 11 pm, Saturday from 11 am to 3 pm and 7 pm to 11 pm and Sunday from 12 noon to 3 pm and 7 pm to 10.30 pm.

Telephone: 01785 284569.

How to get there: Take the A519 and follow it to the village of Woodseaves, which lies to the south of Eccleshall and about 5 miles north-east of Newport. Follow the signs for High Offley and pass the church on the left. Take the next left (Peggs Lane), cross the canal and the inn is on the left.

Parking: The pub has its own car park.

Length of the walk: 2 miles. Map: OS Landranger 127 Stafford and Telford (inn GR 775255).

Quiet country lanes and a stretch of canal towpath make up this very easy but pleasant walk which offers delightful views across spacious, rural landscapes to distant, wide horizons. On the canal bank you might easily find yourself in conversation with the occupants of passing narrow boats – their speed is unlikely to exceed yours!

The Walk

From the inn car park turn right and cross the Shropshire Union Canal. Follow Peggs Lane beside the entrance to a house called Old Lea Wharf and continue between hedgerows. The houses of High Offley can be seen in the distance. Pass some farm outbuildings and then begin to climb the hill towards the village, hugging a holly hedge as you ascend. The outline of High Offley church, dating back over 700 years, can be seen at this point. From the high ground near the church the mountains of Wales, as well as parts of neighbouring Shropshire, can sometimes be seen.

Look for a footpath on the left and right just before the lane curves to the left. Take the right-hand path, climbing some steps to a stile in the hedgerow. Go straight across the field, with the church close by on the left, and enjoy all round views over open farmland. Look for a stile to the left of a large white house and go out to the road. To visit High Offley village, turn left and go up the hill. The Royal Oak is on the corner at the next junction, with the church adjacent to it. To continue the route of the walk, turn right on leaving the field and walk down the lane, passing The Old Parsonage and continuing between banks and high hedges. Further on, the lane makes a wide curve to the right. Pass Yew Tree Cottage and several other houses and continue along the narrow lane. High Offley can clearly be seen if you glance back towards the northerly skyline. Cross the bridge at the hamlet of Grub Street and turn immediately right to join the towpath on the southern bank of the Shropshire Union Canal. The surroundings are thickly wooded and very pretty on this stretch of the waterway.

Keep to the path, the trees soon giving way to reveal views over open countryside. Keep going beside the canal and gradually the pub edges into view. Caravans can also be seen along here and narrow boats are often moored just below the inn garden. Turn left at the bridge to reach the car park.

Places of interest nearby
Izaak Walton, the famous angler, lived at *Shallowford* to the east of Eccleshall. His cottage is now a museum dedicated to the memory of this great figure. The interior of the cottage illustrates the living and working conditions of a typical house of the 17th century, and there are also displays which show the literary and social life of Izaak Walton. The history of angling through the centuries is also recorded. The museum is open during the summer months. Telephone: 01785 760278.

13 Gnosall
The Royal Oak

There is Gnosall and neighbouring Gnosall Heath – the G is silent – and the two communities are bisected by the old Stafford to Newport railway line, which was discontinued in 1964. The old line, in common with many other former railway routes around the country, has been attractively converted into a recreational path and cycleway. The Stafford to Newport Green Way, as it is known, lies just a few yards from the start of this walk.

The Royal Oak, which is located between Gnosall and Gnosall Heath, attracts a good deal of passing trade – hardly surprising as it is on the busy A518 road. Its close proximity to the Shropshire Union Canal means that it is also very popular with boating enthusiasts. The precise date of when it was built is not clear but it is understood to have been a coaching inn at one time. A weekly cattle market used to be held here every Wednesday and the present landlord has records which indicate that cattle sales took place as recently as 1934. Inside, the pub is very quaint with a cosy bar and lounge. There is also a function room.

There is a good choice of food, including a selection of starters, such as soup of the day, deep-fried Brie wedges and garlic mushrooms. Among the main courses are breaded plaice, wholetail scampi, lasagne and Cajun butterfly chicken breast. One of the most popular dishes is the enormous Royal Oak Grill – consisting of a fried egg, 4oz rump steak, 4oz gammon steak, 2 sausages, black pudding, pork chop, 3oz liver, and served with mushrooms and grilled tomatoes. There are also vegetarian dishes, cold platters, a specials board, a children's menu and a range of sweets. On Sunday a traditional roast is served. Tetley Bitter and Burton Ale are available on hand pump and there is also Olde English cider, Kilkenny Irish Bitter and Guinness on draught. Lagers include Lowenbrau, Skol and Castlemaine XXXX.

The Royal Oak boasts a beer garden and a children's play area, and dogs are permitted but only in the bar and on a lead. The inn is open from 11.30 am to 3.30 pm and 6.30 pm to 11 pm Monday to Saturday and from 12 noon to 3 pm and 7 pm to 10.30 pm on Sunday. Food is served from 12 noon to 2.30 pm and 6.30 pm to 9.30 pm (7 pm on Sunday). Large groups are asked to book in advance.

Telephone: 01785 822362.

How to get there: Take the A518 between Stafford and Newport. The pub is on the main road, between Gnosall and Gnosall Heath.

Parking: The inn has its own car park.

Length of the walk: 2 miles. Map: OS Landranger 127 Stafford and Telford (inn GR 826204).

This short walk passes through residential Gnosall Heath to reach the Shropshire Union Canal at Cowley Tunnel. The route then follows the towpath as far as the Stafford to Newport Green Way, returning to the inn along the disused, tree-lined trackbed.

The Walk
From the inn turn sharp right into Wharf Road and pass Cowley Lane on the left. There are other turnings on the left and right which you should ignore. Continue between houses and bunga-lows and pass a bakery on the right, followed by a row of striking

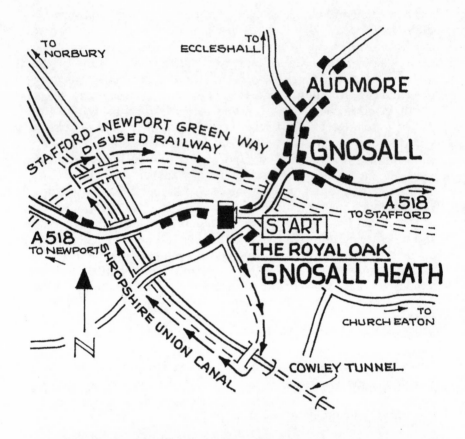

terraced houses. Turn left into Monk Walk and follow the road through the estate, then where it bends right at a sign for Impstones, go straight ahead, keeping to the right of some lock-up garages.

Make for the far right-hand corner of the garage area and look for a sign stating 'Quarry Nurseries, wholesale only'. Join a path and follow it as it bends left along the edge of some woodland. Quarry Nurseries can be seen on the left and soon the outline of the old quarry is visible beyond the fence. Cross the roof of Cowley Tunnel and the Shropshire Union Canal can be seen far below you, cutting through the trees. Turn right at a junction with a track and follow it for a short distance until you come to a stile in the right-hand boundary. Cross over and then head through the trees to join a paved path running down the bank to the towpath. Cowley Tunnel, hewn out of a wall of solid sandstone, looms large as you look to the right. The towpath runs through the tunnel and, if time permits, you may like to make a short detour and follow the canal to the other end. It is dark and dank inside the tunnel; walking through it, as I did, is a curious experience.

Retrace your steps along the towpath and continue in a north-westerly direction. The canal runs prettily between trees and on the opposite bank you can see some distinctive timber chalets overlooking the waterway. Shortly, pass some modern houses and apartments and an iron milepost. Ahead of you now is a curving stone road bridge (Pave Lane Bridge) and on the right at this point is an inn called the Boat, which has been in constant use since the Shropshire Union Canal, or 'The Shroppie' as it is more commonly known, was opened in the 1830s. The 66-mile long canal, famous for its long wooded straights and deep scenic cuttings, was designed and built by the engineer Thomas Telford, though it proved to be very expensive and at times difficult to construct. There were frequent landslips and Telford was forced to make several costly diversions.

The Shropshire Union Canal.

Follow the towpath to the next road bridge (A518) and on the left you can see another pub – the Navigation. Continue on the towpath as it curves to the left. Moored cabin cruisers and narrow boats can often be seen on this stretch of the canal. Walk along to the old railway bridge, pass under it and then bear immediately left up some steps to join the route of the Stafford to Newport Green Way. Turn left, cross the Shropshire Union Canal and then follow the old trackbed between the trees. Keep going along the embankment which affords pleasant views across fields and paddocks. There may be the odd glimpse of a narrow boat on 'The Shroppie' as well.

Ahead of you on the horizon is the tower of Gnosall's stately Church of St Lawrence, considered to be one of the finest in Staffordshire. Parts of the church date back to 1080. Huddled around it are the buildings of Gnosall village, first mentioned in the Domesday Book as Geneshall. On the right of the path are the older houses of Gnosall, many of them Edwardian and Victorian. Continue until you reach some grassy mounds, then bear right to a gate leading out to the road. Turn left and return to the inn. Just before you reach it, look for a fascinating illustrated framed map of Gnosall in years gone by, which includes old photographs of the church, the lock-up and Cowley Tunnel.

Place of interest nearby
Weston Park, the family seat of the Earls of Bradford for 300 years, includes many attractions for the family. The house contains a collection of paintings, tapestries, furniture, porcelain and silver. In the park, designed by 'Capability' Brown, there are many things to see and do – among them, a woodland adventure playground, pets' corner, miniature railway, tropical house and various walks. Telephone: 01952 850207

14 Hoar Cross
The Meynell Ingram Arms

Hoar Cross is a scattered community in the glorious wooded country of the Needwood Forest, once a royal hunting reserve for kings. At the heart of Hoar Cross lies a famous inn, the Meynell Ingram Arms, which takes its name from the Meynell (pronounced Mennell) Ingram family who lived at nearby Hoar Cross Hall during the second half of the 19th century. The inn dates back to the early 16th century and was originally known as the Shoulder of Mutton.

The Meynell Ingram Arms, which features two traditional bars and cosy log fires in winter, has a fine reputation for food and among the starters and light snacks available at lunchtime are home-made soup, creamy garlic mushrooms, Welsh rarebit with egg, mustard and stout, and a wide selection of sandwiches. For something more substantial you could choose gammon steak with fried eggs or fresh pineapple, 8oz rump steak, halibut steak, breast of chicken or loin chops. There are also several ploughman's lunches, a selection of daily vegetarian meals and a specials board, as well as a limited choice of children's meals, a traditional Sunday lunch and an extensive evening menu available in the Deer Park Restaurant, for which it is advisable to book. Real ales include Marston's Pedigree, Adnams Southwold and Boddingtons. Also available on draught are Strongbow cider, Murphy's Irish stout and a choice of two lagers – McEwan's and Stella Artois

There is a very pretty courtyard and garden where families can relax in the summer months. Dogs are permitted inside. Live music is a popular attraction at this historic pub and the Courtyard Bistro Bar is a favoured function venue. The inn is open from 12 noon to 3 pm and 6 pm to 11 pm Monday to Friday, 12 noon to 11 pm on Saturday and 12 noon to 5 pm and 7 pm to 10.30 pm on Sunday. Food is available from 12 noon to 2.30 pm and 7 pm to 9.30 pm Monday to Saturday. On Sunday bar meals are served from 12 noon to 1.30 pm in the bar and from 12 noon to 2.15 pm in the dining room. No food on Sunday evening.

Telephone: 01283 575202.

How to get there: Follow the A515 between Ashbourne and Lichfield and turn into Brakenhurst Road at Newchurch, heading west to Hoar Cross. The inn is in front of you at the next crossroads.

Parking: There is a spacious car park at the side of the inn.

Length of the walk: 3 miles. Map: OS Landranger 128 Derby and Burton-upon-Trent (inn GR 133233).

What sounds like the ghostly echo of royal huntsmen can sometimes be heard in the distance on this glorious walk through the Needwood Forest. The circuit, which also takes in one of Staffordshire's most beautiful churches, offers constant views across rolling, semi-wooded landscapes.

The Walk
From the front door of the inn turn left to the junction and go straight across into Brakenhurst Hill, signposted Needwood. Follow the road over the brook and continue between fields and paddocks. Pass a white cottage and a stile and cross another stream. Head towards an area of dense woodland, pass a pond on the left

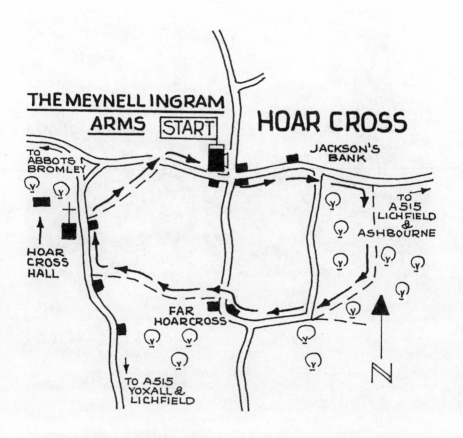

and a turning on the right and continue up the hill, the road climbing quite steeply between lines of oak and sycamore trees. Further up, pass a sign for Jackson's Bank, part of the Duchy of Lancaster and continue on the road for about 75 yards until you reach the woodland edge, then look for a gateway on the right, located opposite a stile.

Bear right and follow the track along the field edge, skirting the forest which lies to your right. In the field corner go through a gateway and proceed straight on into the woodland for about 50 yards, then veer right at the fork. There are few designated public rights of way in this part of the forest, but public access to an extensive area of woodland has been granted by the Duchy of Lancaster in an effort to encourage visitors to roam freely among

The view from Hoar Cross Church.

the trees. Follow the path as it curves to the left and go down the slope to a junction of tracks and paths. Turn right and walk along the track through the trees, with fields soon coming into view on your left. Pass under some pylons to reach the road on a bend, bear left and shortly pass a large house with a conservatory, soon to reach a ford. Cross it by the footbridge and then follow the lane up to a junction, with a farm on the right. Turn right and follow the lane as it bends to the right. Bear left at the entrance to the next farm and then veer over to the right.

Keep a barn alongside you on the right and make for a gate ahead. Proceed diagonally up the field to the top right corner. Hoar Cross church is visible against the wooded horizon. Cross the next field diagonally, aiming for the far end of a line of trees, then bear left and walk up the field with trees and hedgerow on your left. There are far-reaching views over the Needwood Forest at this point. Follow the field edge until you come to a stile taking you out to the road. Turn right and keep the woodland vistas on your right. Pass a postbox and then a striking black and white timber-framed lodge, opposite which is Hoar Cross church, its huge, cathedral-like proportions catching you by surprise. Sometimes described as the most beautiful modern church in England, this magnificent sandstone building, with an embattled central tower, dates back to the 1870s and was the inspiration of Emily Meynell Ingram, daughter of the first Viscount Halifax, who was widowed after only eight years of marriage. She commissioned the church, designed by George Frederick Bodley and generally acknowledged as an architectural masterpiece, as a lasting monument to the memory of her husband, Hugo. A little further along the road is the entrance to Hoar Cross Hall, formerly the Meynell Ingrams' home and now a health spa.

Go through a wrought-iron gate opposite the church, pass between some trees and then veer diagonally down the field slope to a stile at the bottom, among the trees and bushes. Some power lines can also be pinpointed here. Cross the stile and bear immediately left along the field edge, then at the next waymarker veer half-right, cutting off the corner of the field. The houses of Hoar Cross can be seen now, sheltering beneath the wooded backdrop of Needwood Forest. Make for the left side of a black and white building – Hoar Cross Day Nursery – pass through a gateway and follow a drive along to the road. Turn right and return to the inn.

Places of interest nearby
Blithfield Reservoir near Abbots Bromley was officially opened in 1953 and supplies water to a population of 1¼ million in an area of almost 600 square miles. The shoreline and surrounding woodlands of oak, sycamore and beech include a wide variety of plants – marsh marigold, primrose and bluebell among them. The reservoir, an important habitat for many types of birds, is also a popular recreational area, sailing being the main leisure pursuit.

15 Wheaton Aston
The Hartley Arms

Wheaton Aston is a large village, with the feel of a small town, located on the west bank of the Shropshire Union Canal. A fire in the second half of the 18th century destroyed much of the village but, as with many other communities in Staffordshire, it has grown rapidly in size in the last 20 years. The Hartley Arms, once owned by Squire Hartley, is a very popular pub occupying a prime, canalside location. In summer its trade is boosted by boating enthusiasts and those who like to stroll along the towpath.

The menu offers a choice of sandwiches – egg mayonnaise, Cheddar cheese and open prawn – and a range of bar snacks such as beefburger, cheeseburger, jumbo hotdog, salads, ploughman's lunches, various cold platters and filled baked potatoes. There is also sausage, egg and chips, battered cod, breaded plaice, golden scampi, mixed grill, 8oz rump steak, 8oz gammon steak, half a roast chicken and chicken tikka masala. Vegetarians are catered for and there is also a children's menu. On Sunday there is a choice of 3 traditional roasts. Real ales include Marston's Pedigree and Banks's

Bitter, and there is also Grolsh, Harp and Kronenbourg for the lager drinker, as well as Guinness and Strongbow cider on draught.

Dogs are restricted to the beer garden only. The Hartley Arms is open from 12 noon to 11 pm Monday to Saturday and 12 noon to 10.30 pm on Sunday. Bar meals are served from 12 noon to 2 pm and 6 pm to 9 pm, except Sunday evening.

Telephone: 01785 840232.

How to get there: Follow the A5 between Cannock and Telford and follow the signs for Wheaton Aston. Drive through the village and the inn is on the right, immediately before the canal.

Parking: There are plenty of parking spaces at the pub.

Length of the walk: 3 miles. Map: OS Landranger 127 Stafford and Telford (inn GR 855127).

A very pretty path, wooded in places, takes you to the Shropshire Union Canal and then back to Wheaton Aston along the towpath.

The Walk

Leave the inn by turning left and walking along Long Street through Wheaton Aston. Pass various houses and cottages, followed by Caspian Way and Meadowcroft Gardens. Beyond the turnings, veer left into Hawthorne Road and walk along to the roundabout. With the church on your right, bear left and pass Rose Cottage, formerly the mid-19th-century Primitive Methodist Chapel.

Pass Chapel Cottage and follow the lane between picturesque houses. On the right is St Mary's Church of England First School. Continue to the outskirts of Wheaton Aston and keep going along the lane as it crosses a stream and then cuts between hedgerows. The going is rougher underfoot now with muddy patches and frequent potholes. Pass a public footpath on the left and continue ahead on the signposted Monks Walk. The bridleway climbs gently and from the higher ground there are good views over a wide area of rural Staffordshire.

Eventually, where the track bends sharp right, continue straight ahead and go through a waymarked gate. Cross the field to the next boundary, making for a gate by a line of oak trees. Go through the

gate and turn immediately left, following the sign for Lapley. Walk between lines of trees, following the woodland path along the edge of a field. This is one of the prettiest stretches of the entire walk. Beyond the trees, the path continues along the field edge, heading for a gate in the corner. Once through the gate, turn left along a concrete track and after about 50 yards you reach a gate on the right.

Cross the Shropshire Union Canal via the bridge and on the opposite side you will see a sign for the Staffordshire Way. To commemorate the 60th anniversary of the Ramblers' Association in 1995, the Ramblers have co-operated with Staffordshire County Council to carry out repairs to the towpath and erect new signposts.

A narrow boat on the Shropshire Union Canal.

Turn left and go down to the towpath, following it between wooded banks, then after a few minutes the trees give way to views over open fields, with an arched bridge ahead of you. Pass the remains of an old wharf and continue to the lock. Some 160 years ago the newly opened Shropshire Union Canal would have been alive with bargees travelling with their cargoes between London and Liverpool. The scene is quieter now, with various cruisers and narrow boats are often moored on this stretch of the waterway. The Hartley Arms comes into view up ahead. Follow the towpath as far as Long Street, cross the bridge and then bear immediately left to the inn.

Places of interest
Boscobel House, where Charles II sought refuge from Cromwell's soldiers after the Battle of Worcester, dates back to about 1600. In the care of English Heritage, Boscobel House includes an exhibition dedicated to the royal escape of 1651. Telephone: 01902 850244.

16 Slitting Mill
The Horns Inn

Slitting Mill is a pretty hamlet between Rugeley and Cannock Chase, overlooking the valley of the Rising Brook. Many years ago this area echoed to the sound of industry, with a chain of large water-powered mills slitting sheets of iron to produce rods of metal – hence the name Slitting Mill.

The Horns Inn contains several old black and white photographs which depict the pub and the nearby town of Rugeley in days gone by. The inn has changed greatly over the years and now it is a spacious hostelry with a popular menu which also caters well for children. Fresh meat and vegetables are supplied locally. Starters include soup of the day, chicken liver pâté, prawn cocktail and fresh melon. Among the main courses are chilli con carne, steak and kidney pie, golden scampi, chef's chicken curry, 8oz gammon steak, 14oz T-bone steak and 8oz sirloin steak. For a light snack, you could choose from a range of freshly prepared sandwiches, or from ploughman's lunches, salads, jacket potatoes and various sweets. There is also a daily specials board, a choice of vegetarian meals and fresh fish dishes. On Sunday two roasted joints of meat are on offer. Marston's Pedigree and Best Bitter and Banks's Bitter are served on hand pump, with Scrumpy Jack, Strongbow and Woodpecker cider; Foster's, Stella Artois, Beamish stout and Guinness also available on draught.

Outside there is a beer garden and children's play area, with views towards the Horn's Pool. The inn has a Children's Certificate which admits children until 9.30 pm, with children's meals being served until 8.45 pm. Large groups are asked to book at the weekend, especially Sunday lunch. Dogs are not permitted in the pub. The Horns Inn is open from 12 noon to 3 pm and 7 pm to 11 pm (10.30 pm on Sunday) and food is available from 12 noon to 2.15 pm and 7 pm to 9.15 pm.

Telephone: 01889 586000.

How to get there: Follow the A513 to Rugeley. Turn into Hagley Road, north-west of the junction with the A460, then turn left into Slitting Mill Road. The inn is on the left. You can also take the A460, between Cannock and Rugeley, and turn off at the sign for Slitting Mill. The pub is on the right.

Parking: There is a large car park at the side of the inn.

Length of the walk: 3 miles. Map: OS Explorer 6 and Landranger 128 Derby and Burton-upon-Trent (inn GR 028173).

This fascinating walk offers a host of delights. Apart from the wild, unspoilt scenery of Cannock Forest, there is the chance to visit the Birches Valley Forest Centre and learn all about the history and wildlife of this lovely area. The centre, which is open at weekends, includes a shop, refreshments and an adventure playground.

The Walk
From the inn turn left and follow the road, shortly to pass a cul-de-sac and continue along the road, with houses and bungalows on the right and banks of bracken on your left. Pass a row of cottages (Ladyhill Terrace) and drop down the slope beside clumps of gorse bushes. On the right are the trees of Cannock Forest, part of Cannock Chase, a magical landscape of sprawling heather plain and woodland. The area was once a royal forest where Plantagenet

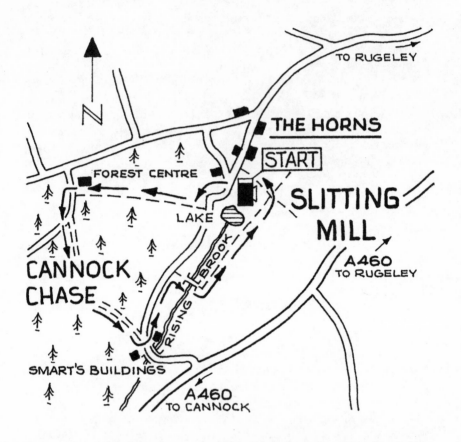

kings hunted game. Its royal status has long gone, but these days Cannock Chase is a delightful, wooded playground much loved by locals and tourists alike and designated an Area of Outstanding Natural Beauty.

At the end of the trees, bear right to join a track. Pass a barrier and walk out across a silent landscape of pine trees and clearings, where the only sound you are likely to hear is the soothing sigh of the breeze stirring the branches. Cannock Forest dates back to the 1920s when many of the trees you see today were planted. The distinctive sandy soil of the area is ideal for the native Scots pine, identified by its reddish bark, and the grey Corsican pine which originated from southern Europe. Fallow deer, badgers and foxes also inhabit Cannock Chase, as does the rather rare red squirrel.

Continue on the track, avoiding all turnings and eventually descend to a major junction of tracks. Do not follow the signposted 'Forest Walk'; instead continue ahead on the main woodland track and soon reach the Birches Valley Forest Centre. Pass alongside the buildings to reach the road and turn left, then immediately beyond a row of houses, veer half-left to join a track, keeping a wire fence on your left. After a few yards the track curves left, with a path running straight on. Keep to the track, go up a slope and shortly you drop down to a junction. Disregard the turning on the right and go straight on, crossing a ford.

Pass a picnic table and benches on the right, ignore a turning on the left at the top of the rise and keep to the right. Follow this very pleasant forest track and soon the trees thin to reveal excellent views across a wide area of Cannock Chase. Descend between trees and margins of bracken to reach the road at Smart's Buildings. Turn left opposite a sign for 'Sheepwash' and a row of houses and follow the road beside lines of beech trees on your left. Pass various houses and bungalows and continue over a gushing stream, the Stony Brook, then, almost immediately, turn right with a footpath sign.

Follow the path to a footbridge over the Rising Brook, then turn left to follow the edge of a large field, with the pretty brook flowing parallel on your left, partly enclosed by trees. Further on, a footbridge takes you over the top of a waterfall; the torrent of foaming water plunging beneath you is one of the unexpected highlights of this walk. Pass alongside the Horn's Pool, an artificial lake created about 200 years ago as a header pool with a force of water powerful enough to drive a millwheel. The lake is owned by the Horns and fishing permits are available at the inn. At the next junction of paths, bear left and follow the sunken woodland path up towards the inn. Finish the walk by turning left into the car park.

Places of interest nearby
Shugborough Hall, the magnificent ancestral home of the photographer Patrick Lichfield, is a few miles away at Milford near Stafford, and nestles within 900 acres of beautiful gardens. The estate, in the care of the National Trust, is one of Staffordshire's major attractions and includes the servants' quarters, a Georgian farmstead and a country museum. Telephone: 01889 881388.

17 Whittington
The Dog Inn

Records indicate that Whittington was a settlement as far back as the 13th century. By the early 19th century the village, a couple of miles south-east of Lichfield, boasted a population of more than 600. Today, 3,000 people live in Whittington, much of its development having taken place during the 1970s and '80s. The Dog was originally a coaching inn and the building dates back about 300 years. Until quite recently the pub was a simple local; however, in 1992 the pub was extended and transformed into a cosy, attractively furnished hostelry with a popular restaurant, panelled bar and good selection of lagers and hand-pulled beers.

Bar meals include several starters, a range of hot platters – home-made chilli con carne, half roast chicken, lasagne, mixed grill and steaks – cold platters and vegetarian main courses. Fish dishes are always very popular – golden plaice, scampi – as are the filled jacket potatoes, salads, rolls and sandwiches. There is also a specials board. The restaurant menu is impressive, with a good choice of dishes. Among the starters are prawn cocktail, pâté, chef's home-made soup and fresh garlic mushrooms. Main courses range from 8oz fillet steak, Dover sole and poached chicken breast to poached halibut steak and mixed grill. There is a selection of puddings and a traditional 4-course Sunday roast. The inn offers 6 real ales – Tetley Bitter, Bass, Ind Coope Burton Ale and Ansells Bitter being among them. Castlemaine XXXX, Skol, Carlsberg Export and Pilsner are also available, as are Guinness and Olde English and Copperhead draught cider.

Overnight accommodation is offered in 6 bedrooms. Dogs are restricted to the garden, where there are tables and benches. The bar is open from 11 am to 3 pm and 5 pm to 11 pm from Monday to Friday (6 pm on Saturday) and 12 noon to 3.30 pm and 6 pm to 10.30 pm on Sunday. Food is available from 12 noon to 2.30 pm and 6 pm to 9.30 pm Monday to Saturday and 12 noon to 3 pm and 6 pm to 9 pm on Sunday. It is a good idea to book for the restaurant at the weekend.

Telephone: 01543 432252.

How to get there: From Lichfield follow the A51 towards Tamworth and turn off at the sign for Whittington. Pass the church and the inn is on the left at the next crossroads.

Parking: There is a car park at the inn.

Length of the walk: 3½ miles. Map: OS Landranger 128 Derby and Burton-upon-Trent (inn GR 162083).

From Whittington the walk heads across country to reach the Coventry Canal. The road, canal and railway line all converge at the little hamlet of Huddlesford, where you join the towpath. The return leg is beside the canal, all the way back to Whittington.

The Walk

From the car park turn right, then right again into Main Road. Pass Milestone Antiques and bear left into Chapel Lane. Follow the lane round to the right and at the next junction, turn left into Back Lane. After about 100 yards bear right at a stile, go across a small enclosure of coarse grass and scrub to the stile in the corner. Follow the field edge, with hedgerow and neo-Georgian houses on your immediate left.

HUDDLESFORD

TO A38 &
FRADLEY

TO
LICHFIELD

COVENTRY CANAL

TO A51,
LICHFIELD &
TAMWORTH

WHITTINGTON

START

THE DOG

TO
ELFORD
&
HARLASTON

Cross several field boundaries, walk alongside a brick wall and continue until you see a stile over on the right-hand side of a paddock. Cross the stile and a footbridge, bear left through a gateway and turn right to join the road on a bend. Turn right and walk away from Whittington, passing the village sign. Follow the lane, which can get busy at certain times of the day, and look back for some memorable views over the rooftops of Whittington. On the horizon ahead of you are the buildings of Lichfield, clustered around its famous Cathedral. Its distinctive three spires are known as the 'Ladies of the Vale'.

Walk down the road to a white cottage and a farm. Just beyond the buildings bear half-right on to a bridleway, heading towards a bridge over the Wyrley and Essington Canal. Lines of cruisers and narrow boats can be seen down below, moored along this stretch of the canal. Continue along the path and follow a field boundary beside a row of oak trees, eventually reaching the road. Turn right, pass the entrance to Lichfield Cruising Club, then go downhill and under the railway line. Follow the road along to the canal bridge, where on the right you will find the Plough Inn. Turn left opposite the pub and go down to the towpath of the Coventry Canal, which is 38 miles long and was completed late in the 18th century. Bear left, go under the road bridge and pass a willow tree in the garden of the Plough. Walk under the railway line once more and soon you come to an information board telling you, in some detail, about the history of the Coventry Canal and other waterways in this part of the Midlands. Pass the lattice windowed junction house of the Lichfield Cruising Club and continue along the towpath.

The canal cuts between fields and in places the scene is quite pretty. Further on, you begin to curve to the right as the waterway approaches Whittington. Follow the towpath beneath various bridges, with the houses of the village on the right and views over open farmland on the left. Pass under the boughs of some willow trees, go under another bridge (no 78) and shortly reach a stone plaque on the left. Sponsored by the Lichfield branch of the Inland Waterways Association, it was unveiled in 1990 to mark the joining of the Birmingham and Fazeley Canal and the Coventry Canal at the Whittington Brook 200 years earlier in 1790. Continue to the Whittington Bridge, leave the canal and go up to the road. Turn right and walk back to the inn. Pass Cloister Lodge and St Giles' Hospice, officially opened by HRH Princess Alexandra in 1983, and return to the Dog, located opposite Whittington Social Club.

Places of interest nearby
Museum of the Staffordshire Regiment at Whittington Barracks has displays of uniforms, weapons and campaign relics. The medals display includes eight of the thirteen VCs awarded to men of the Regiment. Telephone: 01543 433333 extension 3240. *Drayton Manor Park and Zoo* near Tamworth has so many attractions, including rare breeds and a children's corner, that you could easily spend a whole day here. Telephone: 01827 287979.

18 Kingswood
The Summer House

The Summer House is literally right on the Staffordshire/ Shropshire county boundary and its distinctive, black and white timber-framed façade is familiar to many motorists who regularly drive along the A464 Telford road. Its location is rather isolated, the nearest villages being several minutes' drive away.

The inn, which includes a dining area and conservatory, tends to attract a mixture of local customers and passing trade, though it is also very popular with families. There is a function room and carvery, both of which are available to hire. The menu offers a selection of traditional, home-cooked food and among the dishes are various steaks – T-bone, rump, fillet and sirloin. The Summer House grill is also very popular, as are chicken Kiev, lasagne, trout, salmon and a selection of curries. Lighter meals include soup of the day, various salads, a choice of sandwiches and baguettes and a selection of jacket potatoes. There is a traditional Sunday roast in the carvery and a children's menu which includes beefburger and jumbo hotdog. The Summer House is a Banks's pub and so the two beers on hand pump are their Mild and Bitter. Lagers include Grolsh, Harp and Kronenbourg, and there is also Guinness and Strongbow cider on draught.

There is a beer garden and children's play area; dogs are permitted in the conservatory only. The inn is open from 12 noon to 3 pm and 6 pm to 11 pm, Monday to Friday, 12 noon to 11 pm on Saturday and 12 noon to 10.30 pm on Sunday. Food is served from 12 noon to 2 pm (4.30 pm on Sunday) and 7 pm to 9 pm.

Telephone: 01902 372337.

How to get there: From Wolverhampton follow the A41, branching off to join the A464 at Kingswood Common. The inn will be found on the right after about 1 mile.

Parking: There is plenty of room to park at the pub.

Length of the walk: 4 miles. Map: OS Landranger 127 Stafford and Telford (inn GR 831024).

Much of this attractive walk is within the boundaries of Wrottesley Park, popular with visitors and local people who come here to savour its striking vistas and pretty parkland scenery.

The Walk

On leaving the Summer House turn left and follow the main road for nearly 100 yards, before crossing over to join a bridlepath leading into the woods. Follow the path between trees and carpets of undergrowth and on the right, there are glimpses of open fields either side of the county boundary. Keep to the edge of the woodland and shortly pass alongside some chalets and mobile homes.

Continue to a junction of tracks and turn right. Pass a pair of semi-detached houses and a sign – 'private road-public bridleway only. Dogs to be kept on leads at all times', then follow the tarmac drive as it threads between fields towards Wrottesley Lodge Farm. There are very good views across Staffordshire and Shropshire on this stretch of the walk. Pass under some pylons and approach the imposing Georgian farmhouse and its extensive farm outbuildings. Continue on the track, with a bungalow on the right, and head towards a patch of woodland. Keep a wire fence on your left, pass

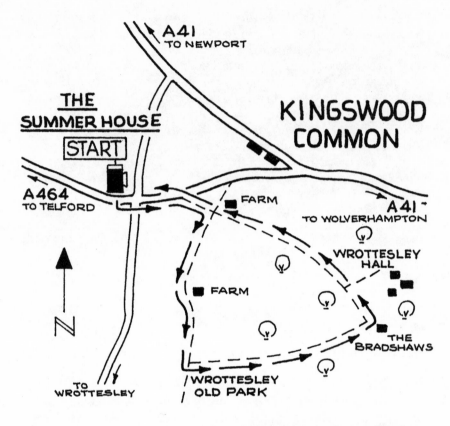

alongside the trees and head for the next area of woodland up ahead.

About 50 yards before you reach the trees, turn left to join a clear track running along the edge of a field. Pass under some pylons and in front of you now are striking views across Wrottesley Park. Continue to the field corner, where you join a track on a bend, and proceed straight on, keeping to the right of a wood. Follow the track, the trees soon giving way to views of the park, pass a finger of woodland on the right and keep going towards some barns and farm outbuildings, part of Wrottesley Park. For many centuries this sprawling estate was owned by the Wrottesley family; these days, however, the accent is on leisure and business enterprise, with the former park now comprising a golf course, market garden and several farms.

Over to the right is the site of a medieval village and moated manor house long since gone. During the Civil War the manor was garrisoned by Parliamentary forces who demolished estate workers' houses to help strengthen its defences against attack. Keep to the left of the buildings and follow a wide track. Pass a bridleway sign pointing straight on and follow the broad drive as it sweeps round to the left. Wrottesley Hall lies to the right, concealed by woodland.

As the drive curves right, go straight on by some larch trees and follow a stony track through the stately parkland. Where the track bends right, proceed straight ahead through a gate to walk along a delightful bridlepath lined by oak trees. Go through another gate and then join a clear track, following it between banks of bracken, brambles and trees. Pass alongside a white house and then continue along the track to the next junction. Go straight across and then retrace your steps along the woodland path and back to the A464. Turn left and return to the inn.

Places of interest nearby
Chillington Hall, near Brewood, has long been the family seat of the Giffard family. The present hall is 18th-century and the parkland was landscaped by 'Capability' Brown in about 1730. There is a spot in the grounds of Chillington Hall known as 'Giffard's Cross'. This is where Sir John Giffard is supposed to have killed a panther with an arrow from a crossbow. Chillington Hall is open to the public during the summer. Telephone: 01902 850236.

19 Wombourne
The Round Oak

Wombourne, which takes its name from the Wom Brook, has expanded in all directions over the years and many of its residents commute to neighbouring towns and cities, such as Wolverhampton and Birmingham. The village centre has survived the years of development, and the parish church, with its 15th-century spire and red sandstone tower, is worth a look.

The Round Oak is situated at the western end of the village, beside the Staffordshire and Worcestershire Canal – probably more commonly known as the Staffs and Worcs. The site of this inn is a popular spot with locals, families and those who spend their leisure time on the water. Even in winter, narrow boats ply the canal. Owned by Banks's Brewery, this pub dates back about 200 years and is a listed building. During the early 1990s the inn assumed a completely new look, when it was enlarged and refurbished. Its spacious but inviting interior and Victorian-style décor draw many new customers. There is the added attraction of a family room with games and videos.

Food features strongly at the inn and the various categories on the menu are reminders of the pub's canalside position. 'Locks Open' includes soup of the day and prawn cocktail; 8oz and 6oz rump steak are among the 'Bargee's Grills' and you can look at a blackboard for a choice of dishes known as 'Narrowboat Specials'. There are also fish dishes, savoury favourites and vegetarian meals, as well as a selection of sandwiches, salads and snacks. There is a separate menu for children under the age of twelve and a traditional Sunday lunch is also available. Several Banks's beers are available on hand pump; lagers include Harp, Grolsh and Zamek, a popular Czechoslovakian brand. There is also Guinness, Woodpecker and Strongbow cider on draught.

The inn has a beer garden and a children's play area. Dogs are restricted to the patio only. Opening times in winter are 12 noon to 3 pm and 5.30 pm to 11 pm Monday to Friday, all day on Saturday and 12 noon to 3 pm and 7 pm to 10.30 pm on Sunday. In summer the hours are 12 noon to 11 pm from Monday to Saturday and 12 noon to 10.30 pm on Sunday. Food is served from 12 noon to 2 pm and 6 pm to 9 pm and there is also a barbecue on summer weekends. Large groups are asked to book.

Telephone: 01902 892083.

How to get there: From Wolverhampton head south on the A449. Turn right at the junction with the A463 and then left at the next main junction. Follow the road, passing a turning to Wombourne centre on the left, and continue straight on at the traffic lights. Pass the New Inn at Wombourne and keep going for nearly a mile to reach the Round Oak.

Parking: There is a large car park at the side of the pub.

Length of the walk: 3½ miles. Map: OS Landranger 139 Birmingham (inn GR 864932).

Those who recall the great days of steam travel will enjoy this fascinating walk in South Staffordshire. The outward leg follows the towpath of the Staffs and Worcs Canal and then returns to Wombourne along a stretch of the Kingswinford Railway Walk, managed by South Staffordshire Council's Ranger Service.

The Walk

From the front door of the pub, go down the steps to the towpath at Houndel Bridge and turn left. Walk alongside the pub garden, passing under the branches of some willow trees. The Staffs and Worcs Canal, engineered by James Brindley and opened in 1722, cuts between fields and patches of scrub. There are glimpses of pretty countryside and areas of woodland in the distance, and the houses of Wombourne can also be seen from here. Up ahead is an angled bridge and a white cottage overlooking the charmingly named Bumblehole Lock. Locally quarried sand was once loaded onto boats here before being transported to foundries and used for moulds in iron castings. On the left is one of a chain of circular side weirs which are unique to the Staffs and Worcs Canal. The side weir was designed by James Brindley and takes up less room than the more conventional system of regulating the flow of water.

The surroundings become increasingly more rural as you progress along the canal towpath, with views across green hummocks to the wooded horizon. Pass a sign 'welcome to Bratch Locks' and continue past a line of bungalows. On the opposite bank is an amenity area and beyond it lies the distinctive Bratch pumping station, famous for being designed in the Victorian Gothic style. With its red, blue and buff bricks and its four corner turrets, it has often been likened to a Scottish castle or a French château. The station, opened in 1897 to celebrate Queen Victoria's Diamond Jubilee, was built as close to the canal as possible so that coal used to fire the two steam engines could be transported by barge. Continue under Bratch Bridge to Bratch Locks. The history of the canal is recorded here and the striking octagonal tollhouse, with its central stone chimney, is one of the highlights of this walk. The Bratch locks are generally acknowledged as one of the engineering triumphs of the Staffs and Worcs Canal.

Cross to the opposite bank of the canal and continue in a north-westerly direction, with the waterway now on your immediate left. Cut through a landscape of scattered woodland, hedgerows and distant hills and leave the towpath at Awbridge Lock. At the road turn left and follow it along to the junction with Blackpit Lane, veering half-right into Flash Lane. Head towards the wooded escarpment on the skyline, pass a turning to Canalside Farm and walk down to the railway bridge. Keep going for about 70 yards, then turn sharp left at the sign for Castlecroft and Wombourne and head up to the Kingswinford Railway Walk, where you turn left.

This old branch railway on the Worcester to Wolverhampton line, dubbed the 'Worse and Worse', was built by the Great Western Railway Company between 1912 and 1925. Its role was to serve the rural communities of Wombourne, Himley and Lower Penn, though it was never a great success and passenger services were withdrawn in 1932. Following the D-Day landings in 1944, it was used to carry casualties of war to hospitals throughout the area. The line later became a victim of the Beeching axe and eventually closed in June 1965.

Follow the path along the embankment, with glimpses of open countryside between the trees and soon reach the buildings of Wombourne Station, which now house a popular tearoom. Follow

The old station at Wombourne.

the walk over Bratch Lane Bridge and continue through a wooded cutting. Pass under a bridge and go on to the next bridge. Keep going for about 50 yards, then turn sharp right and go up the bank between bushes and trees to the road. Turn left and follow the road alongside Ounsdale Road School, then pass Bumblehole Meadows, a residential development, and continue downhill back to the inn.

Places of interest nearby

Baggeridge Country Park is made up of 150 acres of former colliery workings and occupies part of the former Himley Hall Estate, owned by the Lords of Dudley since Domesday. The park is a perfect place to take a stroll and enjoy the fine scenery of South Staffordshire. Telephone: 01902 882605.

20 Stourton
The Stewponey and Foley Arms

Stourton is a large residential village on the western fringes of the great West Midlands conurbation. The village, which lies at the junction of two canals, has expanded greatly over the years and today it is really a suburb of Stourbridge. However, the countryside immediately adjacent to it has largely escaped the planner's axe and is very popular with walkers.

The Stewponey and Foley Arms dates back to the 1920s and is a classic example of an old roadhouse – a large inn or restaurant on a main road in a country area. Changing trends in the pub trade and the influence of a fragile economy have resulted in many of them disappearing over the years. The Stewponey is probably one of the largest roadhouses in South Staffordshire and in its heyday boasted a swimming pool and a grand ballroom, which is now a restaurant where Sunday lunch is served with full silver service (booking advisable).

There is a charming story associated with the inn's unusual name. At the turn of the century a local man went to sea and whilst ashore in the Spanish port of Estepona, he met the daughter of a local bar owner. To win her hand in marriage, he had to promise her father that he would buy her a bar in this country. The man kept his word and bought the Foley Arms, an old inn which had stood on this site for many years. His bride later told a local farmer whereabouts in Spain she had lived and legend suggests that as word spread throughout the community, Estepona gradually became Stewponey.

There is a blackboard menu with several starters – soup, breaded mushrooms and prawn cocktail – main courses include Poney mixed grill, garlic and coriander chicken, gammon steak, rump steak, roast chicken, breaded cod, plaice and scampi. There is also a choice of daily specials, various vegetarian dishes and a children's menu. Banks's Bitter and Hanson's Mild are the two traditional beers on offer; for those who prefer lager, there is Harp and Kronenbourg 1664. Guinness and Strongbow cider are also available.

Outside is a pleasant patio area which is popular with customers during the summer. No dogs please. The Stewponey is open from 11 am to 2.30 pm and 6 pm to 11 pm Monday to Friday, 11 am to 11 pm on Saturday and 12 noon to 3 pm and 7 pm to 10.30 pm on Sunday. Meals are served from 12 noon to 2 pm and 6 pm to 9 pm, except Sunday evening.

Telephone: 01384 872835.

How to get there: From Stourbridge follow the A458 towards Bridgnorth. Pass the sign for Stourton and continue to the junction with the A449. The Stewponey is on the left.

Parking: The inn has a large car park.

Length of the walk: 4 miles. Map: OS Landranger 139 Birmingham (inn GR 863847).

Begin this walk by following a very pretty stretch of the Staffordshire and Worcestershire Canal. An aqueduct and a sandstone cave are among the treats in store. The middle stages reveal pleasant rural views over South Staffordshire and the final stretch of the route is along the towpath of the Stourbridge Canal.

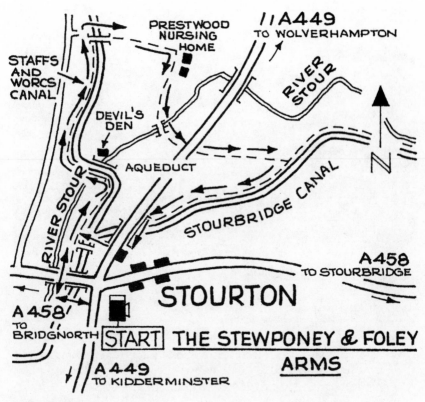

STAFFS AND WORCS CANAL

PRESTWOOD NURSING HOME

//A449 TO WOLVERHAMPTON

RIVER STOUR

DEVIL'S DEN

AQUEDUCT

RIVER STOUR

STOURBRIDGE CANAL

N

A458 TO STOURBRIDGE

STOURTON

A458 TO BRIDGNORTH

START **THE STEWPONEY & FOLEY ARMS**

A449 TO KIDDERMINSTER

The Walk

From the front door go straight over the A449 to join the Bridgnorth road. Cross the Staffordshire and Worcestershire Canal (the Staffs and Worcs) and then bear right on to the towpath at Stewponey Lock. On the left is a circular side weir, only found on this canal, and on the right are several picturesque white cottages – once the toll office and lock-house. Walk along the towpath and on the left is the outline of Stourton Castle, now a bed and breakfast establishment. Pass Stourton bridge and soon reach the junction of the Staffs and Worcs Canal and the Stourbridge Canal. The former was completed in 1722, the latter opened in 1779. Continue along the towpath, following it through a wooded, sandstone cutting, and over on the right, parallel to the canal, is a basin which extends for about 200 yards and was probably used as a distribution point for

The Staffs & Worcs Canal.

local goods. Looking down to the left you will see the river Stour running alongside the canal.

I have undertaken this walk in the depths of winter, watching from the towpath as a fleet of narrow boats carved a passage through the frozen water, great slabs of ice heaving, creaking and finally splintering into smaller shards under the weight of the hulls. Further on, the canal bends to the left, and on the right an arm of the canal can be seen running off to the east. An old design drawing indicates that this was originally intended to be the junction of the Staffs and Worcs Canal and the Stourbridge Canal. However, work was eventually abandoned and the confluence of the two waterways was sited about ½ mile to the south.

Keep on along the towpath and after a few yards you come to the two-arched Stourton Aqueduct, which carries the canal over the Stour. Beyond it you can see the opening of the Devil's Den in the sandstone cliffs across the water. Some sources suggest this cave was used as a shelter by navvies working on the canal, though it may well have been converted to a boathouse for the owners of nearby Prestwood Hall. Follow the canal towpath as it makes a dramatic sweep to the right. Keep going between trees and eventually the woodland thins to offer views over rolling green fields. Ahead of you now is Prestwood Bridge, once described as the most perfect of all the canal bridges. Pass under the bridge, an exact replica of the original one, and then bear immediately left up some steps. Cross the canal and follow a drive past a lodge to Prestwood Hall and alongside a conifer hedge. The drive climbs gently and from the higher ground, there are fine views over open countryside to the east.

Drop down the slope, pass a footpath on the left and the sound of traffic on the A449 is now audible, with trees concealing the road from view. Bear right to join a bridleway, just before a sign for 'Coach House', and follow the path through the trees, then go straight on when you reach a drive. Keep going through the grounds of Prestwood Nursing Home, passing the main buildings on the left and well tended grounds on the right. Pass a parking area, cross the river Stour again and continue on the drive all the way to the road. Go straight over and join a wide track running across the fields, then after about ½ mile you reach the Stourbridge Canal. Turn right and go down the steps to the towpath. Head west beside the canal, following it through a pretty landscape of fields and woodland.

Eventually the houses of Stourton loom into view, some with gardens running down to the water's edge. Pass Stourton Top Lock and continue to the next lock. Cross over to the opposite side of the cut just before the tunnel running under the A449 and follow the southern bank of the Stourbridge Canal to its junction with the Staffs and Worcs Canal. Cross over at Stourton Bridge and retrace your steps to the pub.

Places of interest nearby
Kinver Edge is a fascinating place to visit. The National Trust own 293 acres of wood and sandstone ridge here, as well as various caves and grottoes hewn out of solid rock. Telephone the warden: 01384 872418, or the custodian: 01384 872553.

Other areas covered in the Pub Walks series include:

Bedfordshire
Berkshire
Birmingham & Coventry
Bournemouth & Poole
Bristol & Bath
Buckinghamshire
Cambridgeshire
Cheshire
Chilterns
Cotswolds
Cotswold Way
County Durham
North & West Cumbria
South Cumbria
Dartmoor & South Devon
Derbyshire
Essex
West Essex
Exmoor & North Devon
Gloucestershire
Herefordshire
Hertfordshire
Icknield Way Path
Isle of Wight
Kent
Lancashire

Leicestershire & Rutland
Lincolnshire
North London
Middlesex & West London
Midshires Way
Norfolk
Northamptonshire
Nottinghamshire
Oxfordshire
South Downs
Staffordshire
Suffolk
Surrey
Surrey Hills
Thames Valley
North Wales
South Wales
Warwickshire
Wayfarer's Walk
Wiltshire
Worcestershire
Wye Valley & Forest of Dean
East Yorkshire
North Yorkshire
South Yorkshire
West Yorkshire

*A complete catalogue is available from the publisher at
3 Catherine Road, Newbury, Berkshire.*